A TRAILS BOOKS GUIDE

GREAT IOWA WALKS

50 STROLLS, RAMBLES, HIKES, AND TREKS

LYNN L. WALTERS

TRAILS BOOKS
Black Earth, Wisconsin

Library of Congress Control Number: 2004099152
ISBN: 1-931599-32-7

Editor: Stan Stoga
Design: Kathie Campbell
Photos: Lynn L. Walters
Illustrated Maps: Pamela Harden
Cover Photo: Clint Farlinger

Printed in the United States of America by Sheridan Books

10 09 08 07 06 05   6 5 4 3 2 1

Trails Media Group, Inc.
P.O. Box 317 • Black Earth, WI 53515
(800) 236-8088 • e-mail: books@wistrails.com
www.trailsbooks.com

To my husband, Pat, who walked every trail with me.

Location of Walks

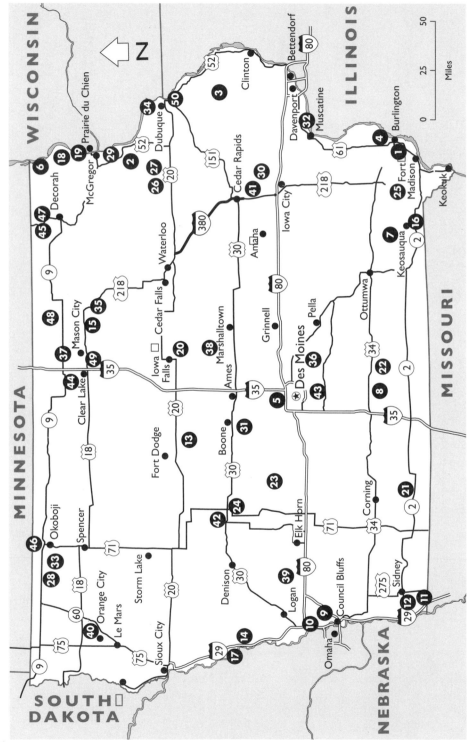

Contents

Loops by Lakes

Overlooks and Vistas

Prairie Paths

Rail Trails and No-Hill Hikes

Springs, Wetlands, and Waterfalls

Urban Strolls

The Hikes at a Glance

	Birds /Wildlife	Cave	Historic	Lake	Overlook/Vista	Prairie/Meadow	River	Waterfall/Springs	Wetlands	Woods/Forest
1. Black Hawk Spring Walk		■	■				■	■		
2. Ice Cave Walk		■			■			■		
3. Maquoketa Caves Walk		■								
4. Starr's Cave Hike		■					■			
5. Neal Smith Trail	■									■
6. Paint Creek Unit Hike	■				■					■
7. Park to Forest Hike	■									■
8. Whitebreast Unit Hike	■									■
9. Badger Ridge Walk					■	■				
10. Overlook Hike					■					■
11. Ridge and Bridge Walk					■					■
12. Vista to Valley Hike	■				■				■	■
13. Boneyard Hollow Hike	■		■		■					
14. Canyon and Prairie Hike					■	■				■
15. Fossil, Kiln, and River Trails			■				■			
16. Lacey-Keosauqua Trails			■				■			■
17. Nature Trails			■							■
18. North Unit Hike			■		■		■			■
19. South Unit Hike			■							■
20. Ancient Pine and Lake Walk	■			■	■					■
21. Lake of Three Fires Hike	■			■						
22. Redbud Walk	■			■						■
23. Springbrook Stroll	■			■						
24. Swan Lake Loop				■						
25. Water and Woodland Walk			■	■						■

Use this guide to help you choose a walk or hike. A feature or sight is marked only if it is significant.

	Birds /Wildlife	Cave	Historic	Lake	Overlook/Vistas	Prairie/Meadow	River	Waterfall/Springs	Wetlands	Woods/Forest
26. Backbone Trail					■		■			
27. East Lake Trail	■			■	■					■
28. Mound Walk					■					
29. Pikes Peak Hike					■		■	■		■
30. River Ramble			■		■		■			
31. Scenic Overlook Trails			■		■					■
32. Wildcat Den Walk					■					■
33. Cayler Prairie Walk	■					■				
34. Goat Prairie Walk					■	■				
35. Juniper Hill and Prairie Trails	■					■				
36. Overlook and Tallgrass Trails						■				
37. Prairie and Wetland Trails	■					■			■	
38. Sand Prairie Stroll	■					■				
39. Old Stone Arch Hike			■							
40. Puddle Jumper Trail						■				
41. Sac and Fox Trail	■		■				■			■
42. Sauk Rail Trail	■		■							
43. Summerset Trail	■								■	
44. Bog and Tower Hike	■				■	■			■	■
45. Malanaphy Springs Stroll							■	■		
46. Marsh, Lake, and Woodland Walk	■			■					■	■
47. Waterfall Hike					■			■		■
48. Wetlands Walk									■	
49. River City Sights			■				■			
50. Riverwalk and Port of Dubuque	■		■		■		■			

Introduction

When I was asked to write a book about walks and hikes in Iowa, I felt like a kid in a candy store. I wanted to include everything! My list of must-do hikes kept getting longer. So I finally put aside my list and hit the trails. I revisited old favorites and got acquainted with some new faces. I talked to hikers and walkers, park rangers, naturalists, and other city, county, state, and national personnel. I plotted out road trips to the four corners of the state—and just about everywhere along the way. And somehow, the list sorted itself out.

To be honest, several walks were a total bust. If I slipped and slid down a trail, couldn't find the correct path, or walked across broken bridges—or forded too many streams without bridges—then I crossed that walk off my list.

And sometimes I was completely blown away. The hike was more than I expected! I walked beneath ancient pines, through prairies awash in color, peered over the edge of bluffs, hiked in a golden forest, waded across streams, and stood beneath a waterfall. Before I finished walking a trail with these highlights, I knew it was a keeper.

Of course, some trails included in this book are more challenging than others. You may have to trudge through mud or scramble up a steep incline to get to the payoff—a gorgeous vista. Other trails offer fantastic sights without any muss or fuss. I've also included no-hill hikes and rail trails—level paths that are fun for everyone. The walks vary from less than 1 mile to 14 miles—and include everything in between those lengths.

Selecting a category for each hike also was a challenge. Many walks could easily fit into two or three categories. A hike listed in the historic section, for example, might have great vistas and woods too. The Hikes at a Glance chart provides a quick overview of each hike, focusing on the features and sights you'll see.

As I completed my hikes, I also realized that city, county, state, and national park personnel are doing a great job with available funds, time, and staff. Their enthusiasm for the great outdoors is catching.

The overall distance for each walk is approximate (as is the time spent walking the trail). You may wish to gawk at scenic vistas longer or walk at a faster pace. Please do so. The maps that accompany the walks reflect the particular trails that I walked, not all the trails at a location. Park maps (and staff) are great resources too. Although the terms "walk" and "hike" are used interchangeably in the book, I did make a few distinctions: shorter distances are walks, for the most part, and the longer treks are hikes.

I hope you enjoy the Ready for More? section at the end of some hikes. It tells you about additional trails at the same location or in the area. You might wish to hike several shorter trails in a day or select longer hikes and spend more time in the area.

Although 50 walks are quite a few to choose from, I wish I could include even more. I'm amazed at how many great hiking spots are scattered across the state. And there are more just waiting to be discovered.

See you on the trails!

Hiking Tips

Ahead of time, fill a box with essential hiking and walking supplies (a tool box works great!). When you're in the mood for a hike, simply throw the box in the car and take off!

Your box should include:
Backpack (lightweight)
Compass/GPS
Disposable rain poncho
First aid kit
Flashlight
Insect repellent
Map
Sunblock

A walking stick or trekking poles also come in handy on rugged terrain.

Also take along:
Bottled water
Snacks (granola bars, fruit, etc.)

To wear:
Cushy socks (wool-blend socks wick moisture from your feet)
Hat or other head covering (a scalp can sunburn too)
Sturdy shoes or hiking boots (I love my low-cut waterproof boots)
Layered, comfy clothing that you can peel off as it warms up

Grab a backpack for longer hikes. Slip in a field guide, along with a few essential items.

Flora & Fauna

Slip a field guide into your backpack or pocket so you can identify what you find along the way. It's amazing how much you'll see on a walk.

Mammals to look for: coyote, red fox, gray fox, raccoon, badger, whitetail deer, woodchuck, muskrat, bat, and more.

Amphibians and reptiles include the leopard frog, painted turtle, snapping turtle, skink, prairie race runner, and fox snake.

From songbirds to waterfowl, birds are abundant on many of the walks. A few of my favorites are the Baltimore oriole, bobolink, indigo bunting, rose-breasted grosbeak, scarlet tanager, great blue heron, and white pelican.

The forests and woods are full of early-blooming forbs. Look for trillium, Dutchman's breeches, red columbine, shooting star, Virginia bluebell, and more. On the prairie, the flowers bloom in waves. And the grasses are lovely even in winter. Look for purple prairie clover, yellow coneflower, pale purple coneflower, leadplant, butterfly milkweed, big bluestem, sideoats grama, prairie dropseed, and more.

And the trees are magnificent. Coniferous and deciduous trees include shagbark hickory, red oak, white oak, silver maple, sugar maple, black walnut, sandbar willow, American elm, honey locust, eastern cottonwood, paper birch, red cedar, white pine, red pine, and many more.

Acknowledgments

Thanks to all the park, preserve, forest, and recreation area employees and volunteers. They sent maps, returned my phone calls, answered questions, visited with me about the trails, and generally made my walks and hikes a little nicer. And thanks to my family members. They walked and hiked with me, made phone calls, and were always on the lookout for a new hiking spot. Katie and Chad explored the caves along the trails, Kevin and Becca climbed hills and shared vistas, and Kris tried out my trekking poles. Kim listened to my stories about the hikes. And Melanie made sure no one bothered me when I was working on "the book."

Thanks to Pamela Harden, who crafted the beautiful maps in this book. And many thanks to my editor, Stan Stoga, and project manager, Erika Reise.

But most of all, thanks to my husband, Pat, who hiked all the trails with me (some more than once), carried the backpack, the GPS, *and* my camera—and always tucked a few granola bars in the pack. He took charge of the maps, directions, and more. Truly, I couldn't have completed this project without him.

Caves and Caverns

Maquoketa Caves State Park

Black Hawk Spring Walk
Crapo Park

Distance: 0.52 mile

Time: 30 minutes

Path: Gravel, dirt, stone, some steps. This short but sweet walk takes you to a clear spring, a cavern, and along limestone bluffs in Crapo Park.

Directions: From Madison Avenue in southeast Burlington, turn east onto Main Drive in Crapo Park. You can park near the Hawkeye Log Cabin.

Contact: Burlington Parks and Recreation Department, 704 Dankwardt Drive, Burlington, IA 52601; (319) 753-8117.

Highlights: A crystal-clear spring and a cave with a historical connection to the famous warrior Chief Black Hawk.

Begin your walk near Hawkeye Log Cabin at Crapo Park in the southeastern part of Burlington. Walk in a southerly direction (to the right of the cabin as you're facing it) to the well-worn path that cuts across the grass, and then head into a wooded area. A sign directs you to the downhill path that begins with steps and some gravel. Soon you'll come to a ravine—with a natural table rock across it. Black Hawk Spring is about 50 feet beyond this natural rock crossing. You'll need to wade through shallow water to enter the cave. Once you enter the cavern, ditch your shoes and enjoy the cold, clear spring water as it gurgles and flows across your feet (it's not deep at all).

A plaque embedded in the stone on the outside of the cavern dedicates the spring to a chief who knew the land well: "Named in honor of the famous warrior Chief Black Hawk who with his tribe used this spring when camping in this vicinity." Walk back into the cavern and look out at the bluffs. Perhaps Black Hawk stood in this same spot. Bend down and cup the clear spring water in your hands, a gesture no doubt repeated many times in the past. It's also been said that tribes once searched for flint in the area.

When you're ready, continue on the path beyond the spring. A thick cable literally keeps you on the path that sidles up the side of the bluff, with a drop-off on the other side of the cable. It's a snug fit between the cable and the cliff—but you wouldn't want it any other way.

As you finish this stretch of the trail, keep holding onto the cable,

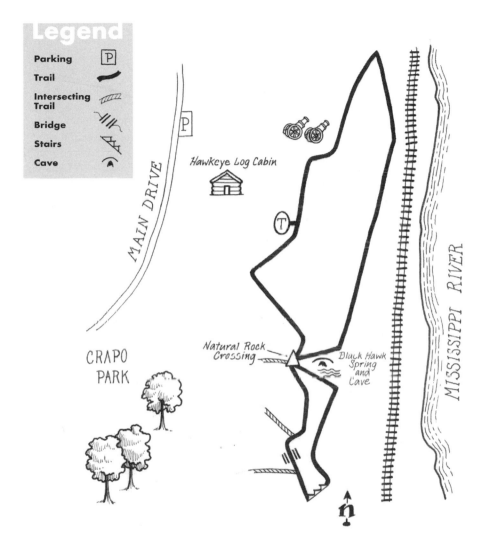

Legend

Parking   P

Trail

Intersecting Trail

Bridge

Stairs

Cave

MAIN DRIVE

Hawkeye Log Cabin

CRAPO PARK

Natural Rock Crossing

Black Hawk Spring and Cave

MISSISSIPPI RIVER

and climb the stone steps carved out of the side of the cliff. Here, a sign indicates that this is the end of the park property. Turn and follow the switchback, up more stone steps in a northerly direction. At the junction just beyond the steps, turn right and cross the ravine via a wooden bridge. You are above the spring now, on a steeper path. At the end of the bridge, another path leads upward, back to where you parked. To the right is a gravel trail on top of the cliff; turn right onto this trail.

Soon, you can hear the spring; look below, and you can see it too. You're above the cave now. At the next junction, you're back at the natural table rock that you walked across to reach the spring and cavern. This time, cross the natural table rock and turn right (rather than return to the cavern or go up the hill, the way you began the walk). Now, you are on the other side of the ravine (on an upper trail). From here you can see the front of the cavern below you, on your right—and the small waterfall created by the spring as it flows out of the cave. Enjoy the view: rock outcroppings, ferns growing out of the rock. Reach out and touch the limestone bluffs as you walk. Above you, trees lean over the ledge, creating a canopy and shade. A thick cable runs along here, too, creating a barrier between you and the drop-off on the right. Below are railroad tracks, and beyond the tracks (just out of sight) is the Mississippi.

Watch your step along here. You'll have an uphill climb for about 0.3 mile as the path leads into the groomed park area. Just ahead are artillery guns mounted on the hillside. A nearby plaque commemorates this as "the first unfurling of the stars and stripes on this site by Lt. Zebulon Pike . . . who landed here August 20, 1805." Enjoy the panoramic view of the Mississippi here too.

Then head back to your car, parked near the Hawkeye Log Cabin. Step inside the cabin if you'd like a peek at pioneer life (limited seasonal hours). Built in the 1900s by the Hawkeye Natives Association, the Des Moines County Historical Society has preserved this building as a log cabin museum.

Ready for More?
Stroll through the Heritage Hill National Historic District in the downtown area. Enjoy the architectural flair of this grand old neighborhood, then slither down Snake Alley, a well-known landmark. Built as a shortcut in the late 1800s, the tightly coiled alley is the ultimate switchback.

Ice Cave Walk
Bixby State Preserve

Distance: Less than 1 mile

Time: 1 hour

Path: Dirt or no path. Once you cross the creek, you'll find a narrow footpath to the ice cave and the springs. But for the rest of the hike you are on your own! You'll be scrambling for footholds on a steep slope up to Steamboat Rock and Castle Rock.

Directions: As you enter Edgewood, which lies on the border of Clayton and Delaware counties, on State Highway 3, turn north on Franklin Street. The turn is marked with a sign to the preserve. Franklin Street turns into gravel at the edge of town and about a mile later becomes Fortune Avenue. Continue on this road, crossing a small bridge just before the parking area on the east side of the road. The preserve itself is not signed. Notice the stone shelter built into the hillside (by the Civilian Conservation Corps) along with a picnic table and grill.

Contact: c/o Backbone State Park, 1347 129th Street, Dundee, IA 52038; (563) 924-2527. (Bixby State Preserve address: 37894 Fortune Avenue, Edgewood, IA 52042.) www.iowadnr.com/preserves

Highlights: The ice cave is the main draw. Cold air flows from the cave onto talus (rock rubble) to form an algific talus slope. This microclimate supports some rare plants. You can feel the blast of cold air from the cave even in the heat of summer. Springs and unusual rock formations also make Bixby a fun stop.

This is a quiet, secluded area. Be sure to wear long pants for this walk (there are no established trails, just footpaths in some areas). To begin, go past the unique stone shelter built into the hillside by the Civilian Conservation Corps. When you meet up with a shallow stream, Bear Creek, cross it (it's not deep). Waterproof hiking boots come in handy here. Otherwise, step on stones to keep your feet dry.

Past the creek, follow the rugged stone stairs that lead to the ice cave. Even before you step on the first stair, you can feel the cold air rushing from the cave. (Close your eyes; you might think you are in front of an open freezer.) Notice the frosty moisture in the air as you climb the 25 steps. You can peer into the cave, but entering is off limits (a gate blocks the entrance). Even on an 85-degree day, the temperature around the cave stays at about 40 degrees.

More stairs to your right lead above the cave, but these steps are precarious. If you use the steps, please don't stray from the path or cause damage to this slope. After you've admired the ice cave, return to the narrow dirt path below the cave and follow the creekbed to the springs, past wildflowers. Climb over any large tree limbs blocking the path. If you step too far to the left, you might tumble into the shallow creek.

The path ends near the springs. The crystal-clear spring water flows close to the ground in several spots. At this point, turn around and retrace your steps, back over the creek, and head to the shelter building. (You could end your walk here.) At this point, you've walked

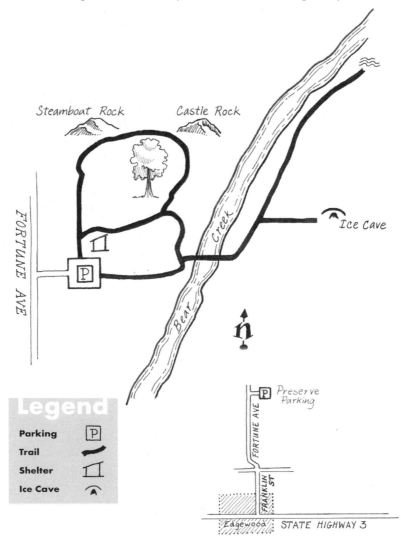

Visitors to the ice cave at Bixby State Preserve are greeted with a blast of cold air.

about 0.5 mile. But if you're ready for a short and steep climb, check out the wooded slope near the shelter house. At the top are some fun rock formations: Steamboat Rock and Castle Rock. Tackle the steep slope any way you can. The remnants of paths you'll find here are not helpful—just confusing. You'll do better on your own. Grab onto tree roots, branches, whatever you can find to make your way up the steep incline.

When you reach the top, enjoy the view into the valley. Look for remnants of the foundation from the Bixby cabin here, too, before scrambling back down. Although this area is mostly mature oak/hickory, notice the huge cottonwoods in the grassy expanse near the parking lot as you return to your car.

Ready for More?

Stop at Backbone State Park (about 15 miles away). You can walk the "devil's backbone" or stroll on trails near the lake.

Maquoketa Caves Walk
Maquoketa Caves State Park

Distance: Slightly less than 1 mile

Time: 1 hour

Path: Boardwalk, stairs (wooden, cement, and stone), and dirt path. This walk takes you down into caves and up some steep inclines.

Directions: Just north of Maquoketa on U.S. Highway 61, turn west onto Caves Road (County Road Y31). After about five miles, turn left at 98th Street and follow this road into the park. Near the lodge, park your car.

Contact: Maquoketa Caves State Park, 10970 98th Street, Maquoketa, IA 52060; (563) 652-5833. www.iowadnr.com/parks

Highlights: The various caves are wide, skinny, tall, squat, spacious, and small. This walk is a great introduction to the caves and the park. Prefer to stay clean—and above ground? Check out the other trails (or just bypass the caves and enjoy the beautiful bluffs). But it won't be as much fun! Take a flashlight.

Start your walk at the stairs directly across the road from the lodge. Pick up a brochure with a park map (and cave locations) from the nearby kiosk if you wish. Check with the ranger if you have questions. Partway down this series of steps (more than a hundred before you're through) is a junction with a dirt path (to other trails and caves) to your left. Ignore it and continue down the boardwalk's wooden steps to the upper entrance of Dancehall Cave, one of three entry points into this long, tunnellike cavern. (Dancehall is more than one thousand feet long.)

Before entering Dancehall, turn left and wander beneath Natural Bridge, a magnificent arch that rises almost 50 feet above Raccoon Creek. Then return to the cave. As you enter, you'll need to crouch for a couple hundred feet, walking along the left side of the cavern. (Minimal seasonal lighting is provided.) Bounce your flashlight beam around and check out the neat cave formations. Keep in mind that fragile formations can be damaged by your touch. Soon, there's enough height to raise your head as the concrete walkway leads you across a small stream to the right side of the cave. Watch for the Bat Passage along here, a modest hole-in-the-wall above eye level. It's a fun passage to explore; go ahead and take a 10-minute side trip here. (Grab a buddy for a leg up to the opening.) When you reach the other

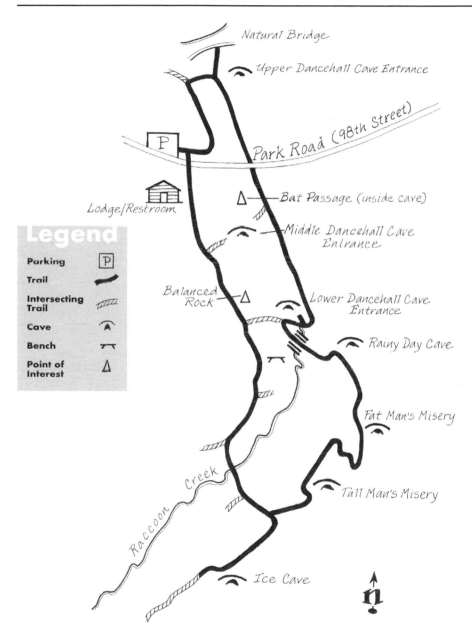

Natural Bridge

Upper Dancehall Cave Entrance

Park Road (98th Street)

P

Bat Passage (inside cave)

Lodge/Restroom

Middle Dancehall Cave Entrance

Balanced Rock

Lower Dancehall Cave Entrance

Rainy Day Cave

Fat Man's Misery

Tall Man's Misery

Raccoon Creek

Ice Cave

n

Legend

Parking	P
Trail	
Intersecting Trail	
Cave	
Bench	
Point of Interest	Δ

end of Bat Passage, there isn't a good spot to jump down, so turn around and wiggle back to your entry point.

Now the walkway takes a sharp right (a flashlight really helps here). Perhaps you'll spot the big brown bat or the little brown myotis. Admire these interesting creatures, but don't disturb them. Bats need their beauty sleep, too! When you arrive at a junction in the walkway, go up about 16 cement steps, turn left, and continue on inside the cave. This is the middle entrance to Dancehall Cave. (Don't take the long flight of stairs; they lead up and out of the cave.)

In winter, up to a thousand bats may stream into this cave and hibernate. A section of Dancehall Cave is off-limits to visitors during this period (usually early November to early April).

Caves of all sizes and shapes are the hallmark of Maquoketa Caves State Park.

Continue on to the large room on your right side, known as the "dancehall." Close your eyes and drift back to a different decade; imagine laughter and music echoing in the cool cavern on a hot summer day, fiddles, and feet flying. Or go back further in the past— Native American artifacts have been found in several of the park's caves. Now open your eyes and walk the "hall," then look ahead: the lower entrance to Dancehall Cave shimmers in front of you. Lush trees, bathed in sunlight, are framed in the entrance.

As you exit the cave, don't take the stairs; continue straight (and then slightly left) on your way to Rainy Day Cave. Walk across the bridge here. The trickling stream below is the same one that flows through Dancehall Cave. Now turn right and climb the 20-plus stairs. Look up at the impressive 70-foot bluff leaning into the trail on your left. Descend about 42 steps to reach Rainy Day Cave. Step inside and check it out (yes, it's wet), then continue on the downhill, rocky path.

Now you're at Fat Man's Misery, a narrow passage called a mechanical cave (major rock movement forms this type of cave). About 18 stone steps lead into this skinny passageway. Don't worry; it's actually large enough for two people to go through side by side. Then, get ready for another passage: Tall Man's Misery, the other mechanical cave in the park. Slip around it or stoop down to step through it.

Soon, there's another junction. Don't take the steps down—continue straight along the bluff. Then climb some stone steps and a few wooden steps to the entrance of Ice Cave. Ahh . . . natural air-conditioning. The cave's cold air is a bonus on a steamy summer day. Cool off, then return to the previous intersection (near Tall Man's Misery). Bear left down the steps and then go straight, continuing on to Balanced Rock (signs point the way). Cross a shallow creek here. Use the stepping stones if you prefer dry feet.

At the next junction, turn right, still on your way to Balanced Rock. Then take a left and climb some stairs. Continue to follow the signs to Balanced Rock, stopping at an overlook with benches. (As you walk along, ignore the junctions on your right that head back to Dancehall Cave.) Then more stairs lead you past the 17-ton Balanced Rock. (Go ahead and lean against it—it won't topple over!) Finish up with about 50 more stairs on this path. Soon you're at the lodge, near your car.

Ready for More?

There are plenty of other caves along the trails (usually 13 caves are open to visitors). If you're ready to be a spelunker, be prepared: wear old clothes (including gloves), shoes or hiking boots with a good grip, and a caving helmet or other hardhat. Take several flashlights (or headlamps, etc.), extra batteries, and a couple of buddies. Caving clubs can be a great source for information—and an ideal way to experience the wonderful world of caves.

Starr's Cave Hike
Starr's Cave Park and Preserve

Distance: 2.25 miles

Time: 1.5 hours

Path: Paved for a short distance (part of an accessible trail), then dirt. And you have a new bridge to cross on your way to Starr's Cave.

Directions: About 5 miles from downtown Burlington on State Highway 61, turn east onto Upper Flint Road. After about 1.5 miles, turn south onto Irish Ridge Road, which leads to Starr's Cave Road and the entrance (west). Park in the lot by the Nature Center.

Contact: Des Moines County Conservation, Starr's Cave nature center, 11627 Starr's Cave Road, Burlington, IA 52601; (319) 753-5808. www.dmcconservation.com

Highlights: Caves and fossils make this a fun hike. The park is a geological preserve as well: unique oolite limestone was discovered in the bluffs here. Look for bats in Starr's Cave (closed during the colder months for hibernating bats). Starr's Cave is the only natural cave at the park: Crinoid Cavern and Devil's Kitchen are both man-made.

Begin your walk at the trailhead north of the center. As you walk toward the trail, notice the large sycamores in the picnic area. Stop at the nature center and chat with the naturalist if you have any questions. The naturalist is a good source of info about the caves, limestone bluffs, fossils and wildlife. Brochures can be found inside the entryway of the nature center (or check the map board at the trailhead). If you visit the park in the winter, rent a pair of cross-country skis from the center and take off on the trails.

In warm weather, listen for birds as you step onto the paved, shaded path (about six to eight feet wide). This section of trail is part of the accessible loop. You may notice other company too: Mosquitoes love this area. Be sure to bring along plenty of insect repellent!

Follow the paved path in a northerly direction to the brand-new accessible bridge that stretches across the creek to Starr's Cave. Gone is the need to ford Flint Creek to reach this cave (although that has been fun).

At the bridge, look across and admire the bluffs (known as Starr's Cave Formation), notable for the oolite limestone discovered here. Notice the horsetail that grows near the creek, flourishing in the low

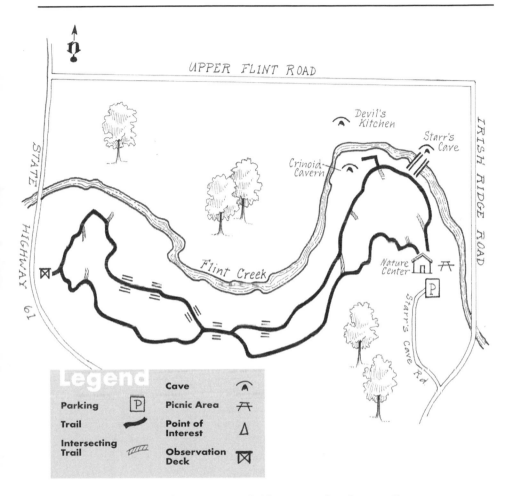

UPPER FLINT ROAD

Devil's Kitchen

Starr's Cave

Crinoid Cavern

STATE HIGHWAY 61

IRISH RIDGE ROAD

Flint Creek

Nature Center

Starr's Cave Rd.

Legend

		Cave	⌃
Parking	P	Picnic Area	⅄
Trail	➔	Point of Interest	Δ
Intersecting Trail	▨	Observation Deck	⊠

area. Then walk across the impressive bridge, a 270-foot-long walkway and platform that will deliver you right into the mouth of the cave.

Carry a flashlight if you wish to delve deeper into the cavern. You can maneuver about 100 yards once inside—and then you may need to "worm crawl" a bit. Look for the little brown myotis or the big brown bat. The cave is closed during the winter to accommodate hibernating bats.

After you've scrambled and squirmed around in Starr's Cave, return to the paved trail and head for Crinoid Cavern, west of the bridge on a dirt path. Climb up a steep incline to the cave, then stand inside and look around this man-made cavern. See if you can spot the Cheerios-shaped fossils embedded in the rocks, sections of crinoids from eons ago when this was still ocean.

Back on the trail, bear right and continue in a southwesterly direction on the dirt path. Notice the wild raspberry in season and the

Virginia waterleaf along here (and plenty of mosquitoes!). Here, it's likely to be muddy—and it's all uphill. You'll see maple and white oak as you walk. Soon, there is a bench near some wild roses and somewhat of a lookout—although it's difficult to see past the trees. At the next junction, continue straight. Notice shagbark hickory through here. Almost immediately, at another junction, turn right. The dirt trail changes from about a foot wide to a grassy trail about three to four feet wide.

At about 1 mile into the walk, within a short distance you'll cross a series of five small wooden plank bridges. Cross the first bridge at a junction; turn right. The second bridge comes up quickly, in a matter of minutes. Then, at the T-intersection, go right. Here, cross three more small bridges. (You'll cross five bridges in less than 0.5 mile.)

Long pants are a good option for this walk, to avoid the poison ivy, which you will see. Notice a trail junction to the right: don't take it—it leads to the creek.

Then, at the next fork in the trail, take a right. This section of downhill path is less traveled and only about a foot wide. Bear right at the next intersection as well. Follow the trail to a platform that overlooks this field/prairie. You've walked 1.5 miles to this point. Retrace your steps to the last fork in the path; this time turn right, up a steep incline. Go right at the next T-intersection too. It's about 0.25 mile until the next junction, where you bear right, just before a bridge. After you cross this bridge, veer right at the junction. Here, you can again see a fence that marks the boundary line. (You crossed these same bridges on the way to the prairie.)

Now you will start on an uphill path again. At about 2 miles, notice the housing development along the boundary line to your right. The trail is grassy now, and you'll see red oaks along here. Listen for cardinals. In a short distance, head back into the woods on a dirt path about five feet wide. At the next junction, go right. Although you will see some trail markers along here, the interpretive trail has not been kept up.

A wild turkey hen and her young scurry across the path. At the next fork in the trail, go right. Now, at about 2.25 miles, you have a short but steep downhill trek as the path winds down to the nature center. Return to the parking area and your car.

Ready for More?

Check with the naturalist to see if the short trail to Devil's Kitchen, a man-made cave on the other side of the creek is open to the public. If so, here's your chance to wade the creek. Durable hiking sandals come in handy—you won't even have to remove them. When you're through exploring, cross the creek and return to your car near the center.

Forest and Woodland Walks

Yellow River State Forest

Neal Smith Trail
Sycamore Access

Distance: 4.8 miles (round trip)

Time: 2.3 hours

Path: Asphalt. You can walk this wide asphalt trail in all seasons. The path rambles through woods, a seasonal wetland, and a meadow. The long hill near the turnaround point keeps things interesting.

Directions: From Interstate 35/80 in Des Moines, get off at Merle Hay Road (Exit 131). Head north until you reach NW 62nd Avenue, then turn right (east). At the intersection of 62nd Avenue and NW Beaver Drive, turn left (north). At 66th Avenue, turn right (east) and travel about 1 mile. Just after crossing the Des Moines River, take a left into the parking area. Signs mark the trailhead, visible as soon as you drive in.

Contact: U.S. Army Corps of Engineers, 5600 NW 78th Avenue, Johnston, IA 50131; (515) 276-4656.

Highlights: Popular trail for hiking and biking. Even when the parking area is full (on weekends), the trail doesn't feel crowded—it goes on for miles. During the week, you'll only see a few runners, walkers, or bikers. In winter, much of the trail is protected from the wind, and you'll have the path to yourself—except for a few deer.

At the trailhead, you'll understand the name: sycamores line the path, jutting into the sky. As you start off on the asphalt trail, listen for the cowbird and watch for the colorful rose-breasted grosbeak. In winter, deer may wander across the path, startled by your presence. The trail stays fairly level until the first junction at about 0.35 mile, where a sign points to the Cottonwood Recreation Area on the left. Don't turn; continue on. The wooded trail gently descends into a lowland area at about 0.5 mile. If you're on the trail near dusk, this is where you'll likely hear a barred owl (sometimes during the day too)—or even the great horned owl.

During a soggy season, the low areas on both sides of the path may be underwater, creating some nice wetlands. In wet weather, leopard frogs frequent this section of the trail, sometimes landing beneath bicycle wheels or a runner's shoe. Here, catch a glimpse of a great blue heron rising from the water or a wood duck hen guiding her ducklings.

Now, at about 0.75 mile, a gradual uphill curves into a more open area. When cottonwood fruits burst, plenty of the white, wispy "cotton" floats through the air. Watch for a streak of blue as an indigo bunting flits near the edge of the wooded area to the left. Along the curve, notice the small stand of pine on the right. You'll also see wild grape here and wild raspberries in season. Late summer, goldenrod and a variety of other golden blooms line the path. This "open" curve drifts over with snow in the winter, although the rest of the trail is fairly protected. (This is a great winter walk too.) The trail curves west for about 0.25 mile.

At 1.35 miles into the walk, you'll come to a junction with a road

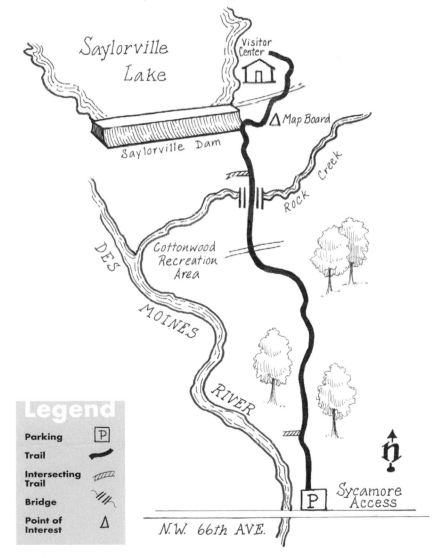

that leads into a recreation area to the left. Don't turn; cross the road and continue on the trail. A pasture (look for horses munching grass) will be on your right. This open area quickly changes back to woods. Note the large silver maples here. Just before you cross a wooden plank bridge, a bench faces the creek. If the weather has been dry for a while, the creekbed will be dry too. Take a short detour—scramble down the riverbank and walk along the bottom, noting the assortment of animal tracks along the way.

Back on the path, just past the bridge is another junction to the left. Ignore it. Here you'll begin a long uphill climb that isn't difficult but seems to go on forever. To the left is another area that, depending on the rainfall and season, is usually wet. White pelicans sometimes stop here in the fall when they migrate—their bright orange bills and black-tipped wings are fun to spot.

Soon you'll feel the effects of the steep incline, so the strategically placed bench at about 1.75 miles is a welcome sight to hikers and bikers who need a break. Past the bench, the trail curves to the east, then back north. In the spring, a nice patch of mayapples appears along here. Mayapples bloom early, to catch the sun before the trees' budding leaves block the light. Note the U.S. Reservoir boundary marker on the right and the red oaks and white oaks lining the trail.

At the top of this long hill, look to your left to Saylorville Dam. At the beginning of your walk, you were below it; now you're at the top, up about 136 vertical feet from the start of the walk. Notice some basswood here, recognizable by its heart-shaped leaves. The trail leads out of the woods and up to the road that passes over the dam. (You could turn around here if you wish.) In late fall through March, bald eagles roost at Saylorville Lake—the dam overlooks are great viewing spots for these magnificent birds. The map board here has lots of Saylorville information, including area activities such as the Pelican Festival at Jester Park in September.

After checking the board, cross the road and go left (north) at the stop sign. The entrance to the visitor center is about 0.25 mile more on your left. Inside, take a look at the wildlife displays; if you need a field guide, purchase one here. You also can go to the lookout point or wander down to the beach. When you're ready to head back, return to the trailhead near the map board (just down the road). Back on the trail, you'll probably grin as you view the long hill—from the top going down this time.

If you're hiking late in the day, time it so that you reach the lowland area just past dusk. Early evenings, June through July (and even into August), fireflies light up the woods, blinking and twinkling all around you. It's such a magical show, you almost expect Tinkerbell to light on your shoulder. Slow down and enjoy! Just remember the bug spray when hiking at night. Take a flashlight too.

Continue retracing your steps until you reach the parking area, where you began this walk.

Ready for More?

About 0.25 mile north of the visitor center, enjoy the butterfly garden—and more miles of trails. Or combine a hike with pelican watching at Jester Park near Granger. In August and early September, you'll see one of the largest migrations of white pelicans in the central states region (as many as 14,000!).

Paint Creek Unit Hike
Yellow River State Forest

Distance: 7.1 miles

Time: 4 hours

Path: Dirt, crushed rock, gravel, grass. Wide, well-marked trails loop and wind through the forest. You'll walk a few sections of park road as well. There are a couple of steep inclines on this hike, but the paths generally meander up and down in a friendly fashion.

Directions: From State Highway 76 about 12 miles southeast of Waukon, turn onto County Road B25, also known as State Forest Road. Follow this road for several miles, past a church and a few intersections. You'll pass by Big Paint Campground on your left, just before an information kiosk (also offering a telephone and water). At the forest headquarters, turn right into the parking area. You'll see a sign for Backpack Trail.

Contact: Yellow River State Forest, 729 State Forest Road, Harpers Ferry, IA 52146; (563) 586-2254. www.iowadnr.com/forestry/yellowriver

Highlights: Yellow River State Forest (Paint Creek Unit) is a great place to get away from it all. Although the entire Backpack Trail system is about 25 miles, various paths wind through the forest, so it's easy to choose a segment or two to hike. Take a 2-mile walk or a 12-mile jaunt—it's up to you.

This forest is fabulous in the fall. Towering pines provide a backdrop for brilliant autumn foliage. The crisp air is invigorating, the mosquitoes long gone, and the trails crunchy with fallen leaves. On breezy autumn days, golden-hued leaves shower from the trees, swirling and skipping down the paths.

Talk with the ranger at the headquarters before taking off into the forest. The ranger can fill you in on the terrain and what to expect on the various trail segments. Some trails have steep inclines, while others are more moderate. Don't guess! Also, carry a compass or GPS. (Bring your daypack with other hiking essentials, including water.) Deep in the forest, one tree looks like another. Be sure to allow enough time to get back to your car before dark.

Start your hike from the parking area. Head south, past the hike-in camping registration board. Maps are here, too, if you didn't pick one up inside the headquarters. The trailhead is marked with a sign on a utility pole. The grassy path starts out about 15 feet wide but narrows and widens throughout the walk.

In a few hundred yards, another sign announces the beginning of the Backpack Trail, which began in August 1974. Several years ago, this trail was named the best hike in Iowa (and one of America's Top 50 Hikes) by *Outside Magazine*. That's a neat endorsement, and after you walk the trails, you'll know it's still true.

Continue in a southerly direction, along the side of a gully (or draw)—across the bottom and back up the other side—past a variety of oaks. As the path narrows, you'll see more dirt than grass beneath the leaves, as well as a few tree roots and jutting rocks. Watch your step. It's easy to trip when you're busy looking at the seemingly end-less forest, spread out before you.

At the first junction, slightly less than 0.5 mile into your walk, turn left, in the direction of the fire tower as marked by the sign. Maples and smaller understory trees also line your path. Near this junction, notice the large rock outcropping to the left, back from the trail. In summer, the outcropping is not as noticeable, but when the trees start shedding their leaves, it pops into view.

Now the easterly trail follows another

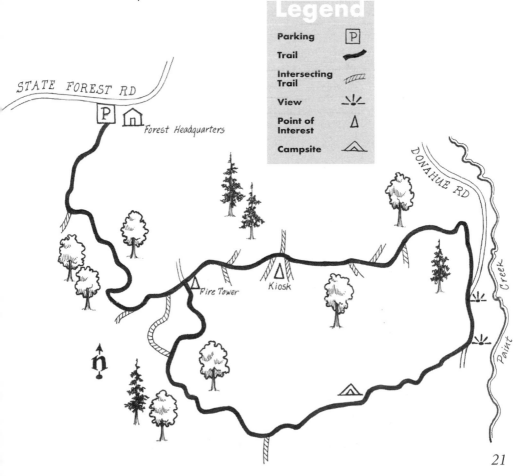

draw. Boulders line one side of the path. Enjoy the gentle up and down of the trail here, because the incline gradually becomes steeper. The path narrows to about three feet, on the edge of a draw. Admire the spectacular fall foliage: multihued maples, rusty-red oaks, and butter-yellow aspens. On windy autumn days, leaves shake loose from the trees like confetti. Wonderful!

Yellow River State Forest (Paint Unit) offers many miles of secluded trails.

In about a mile, you'll reach a signed Y-intersection; bear left. (Camp John Schultz is to the right.) The trail isn't quite as rocky here, and only a few roots and branches lurk beneath the leaves. Now on top of the ridge, you'll get a bit of a break. Notice the shagbark hickory—lots of it. Also notice the ski symbols on posts that mark winter ski trails.

The next well-marked junction (at about 1.25 miles) indicates that Brown's Hollow Camp is to the right and the fire tower is to the left. Turn left. Soon you'll come to a metal gate, followed by an intersection with a gravel road. Turn right onto the road. Huge white pines, planted more than 30 years ago, tower along both sides of the narrow, one-lane gravel road. The tops of these majestic pines almost meet in the middle as they stretch to the sky. Walk this road—which is more like a path—for almost 1 mile. Take advantage of the easy footing here; stretch your stride and enjoy the scenery—and the downhill. The pines keep you company for the next 10 minutes or so.

At about 2 miles into the hike, you'll come to a trail sign and a junction to the right. Don't turn; stay on the gravel road. There are several rock outcroppings on your left. You've lost about 230 feet in elevation as you continue on this road. The composition of the forest is changing; as you descend, take note of the lowland trees.

Now (at about 2.5 miles), you'll come to another junction with a Brown's Hollow Camp sign. Leave the gravel road and turn left onto this flat, grassy trail. Continue past a metal gate and walk through Brown's Hollow Camp. It's a small, secluded clearing with a fire pit and wood to burn—the perfect place to pitch a tent. In autumn, fruit from a prominent walnut tree dots the ground.

As you leave Brown's Hollow Camp, you're still descending. Notice the cottonwood along here—and the waist-high horsetail that is partial to lowlands. Red-headed woodpeckers flit back and forth across the path. Look ahead. The metal gate across the trail signals an intersection with a road. Turn left onto Donahue Road. (You've walked about 3.5 miles to this point.) A small amount of gravel is scattered on this narrow, one-lane road. Here, you'll face a rugged climb. On the edge of the trail, look east, down into a steep ravine. The ravine then rises to a majestic ridge, blanketed with autumn's jeweled colors. Admire the awesome scenery, then continue on this road for about 0.5 mile. Go past an old stone wall that has been torn down on the right.

At about 3.65 miles, Donahue Road intersects with a trail on your left. Before you turn onto this trail, check out the scenic overlook to your right. A large boulder makes a great place to sit and contemplate the view. Note a few scraggly red cedars along here.

Now turn left. Signs indicate that this section of trail is for foot traffic, horses, and bikes. You'll sink into deep gravel with your first step on this steep incline. A few more scraggly cedars line this six-foot-wide path. Look to the right—you can see the road down below and Paint Creek beyond. Watch out for horse droppings along here. Soon you're at the top of a ridge in an open area. You've climbed more than 200 vertical feet on this short, steep incline. Notice remnants of Queen Anne's lace as you head south on the now-grassy path. Although the path runs along the top of a ridge, you're far from the edge—and without a view.

Meander in a westerly direction now, and notice the stand of white pines. You've walked about 4 miles to this point. The grassy trail is about six to eight feet wide. Soon you'll enter a canopy of trees. In about 0.25 mile, an intersection goes to the left or straight. Go straight. You'll notice a small amount of gravel or crushed rock on the trail here. As you leave the trees and head south, back into the open, you'll pass by a food plot to the right. You may notice a ski trail along here too.

Continue on this path, ignoring several intersecting trails as you enter a stand of pines again. Pine litter covers the path, and its sharp fragrance fills the air. The pines lean toward each other across the trail, branches touching. In about 0.1 mile, you'll leave the pines behind, back into the open.

Now, you'll reach a kiosk and map board. Pick up another map or take a break if you wish, then keep going straight on the trail.

At the next junction (you've hiked almost 5 miles to this point), the trail takes off in several directions, with signs identifying the paths, but you will continue to go straight. Look for the sign with the arrow pointing to the direction of the fire tower. After a bit more uphill, it's a gentle downhill as far as you can see. The mix of trees includes maples, oaks, and a few red cedars.

Walk another 0.5 mile to the fire tower. The Evergreen Trail is directly across from the fire tower, to the left—don't take it. Go past the fire tower. Now you're back at a familiar intersection near the beginning of the hike, by the fire tower sign. Cross the road and stay on this trail, as it goes past the gate (the road to the right would also get you back). Retrace your steps, making right turns until you're back at headquarters.

Ready for More?

Return another day and pick other paths. Ask the ranger about the Bluff Trail.

Effigy Mounds National Monument and Pikes Peak State Park are in the area too.

Park to Forest Hike
Lacey-Keosauqua State Park and Shimek State Forest (Keosauqua Unit)

Distance: 4.6 miles

Time: 2.5 hours

Path: Dirt and grass paths. This walk begins in the park on the way to the forest. The trails range from steep and narrow to wide and rolling.

Directions: In Keosauqua, head south on State Highway 1; as soon as you cross the bridge over the Des Moines River, turn right (south) at the entrance to Lacey-Keosauqua State Park. Then follow the park road several miles, past the picnic area, Ely Ford Mormon Crossing, and the lodge. Just past the lodge is a roundabout for parking on the left side of the road (near the park's northwest entrance). Park here.

Contact: Lacey-Keosauqua State Park, P.O. Box 398, Keosauqua, IA 52565; (319) 293-3502. www.iowadnr.com/parks
Shimek State Forest, 33653 Route J56, Farmington, IA 52626; (319) 878-3811. www.iowadnr.com/forestry/shimek

Highlights: Enjoy a peaceful forest walk that begins in the adjoining state park, Lacey-Keosauqua. Deer, owls, and other wildlife are abundant here. Bring a GPS or compass along too.

After parking your car on the roundabout, look to the opening in the trees for the trailhead. Follow the path into the woods; you'll reach the forest boundary in less than 0.5 mile. As you begin, the 15-foot-wide grassy trail quickly changes to dirt and narrows as you head downhill.

Cross the first bridge over a gully in about 0.1 mile. After a rain, the gully quickly fills with water. There are remnants of crushed rock on the trail, which is about four to five feet wide now. The path veers to the left and continues to descend for a short distance before it levels off. Notice that much of the trail is covered with moss.

At the first junction, turn right (a sign says the other path leads to the park road), then cross a bridge over a ravine (this also fills with a lot of water after heavy rains). After the bridge and this grassy clearing, a rather steep uphill climb awaits. Soon (less than 0.5 mile into your walk) you'll reach the forest boundary and a sign that says State Forest/Public Hunting/Wildlife Management Area. Be mindful of hunting seasons; as the sign points out, hunting is allowed.

This natural path is covered with forest vegetation; you won't see

25

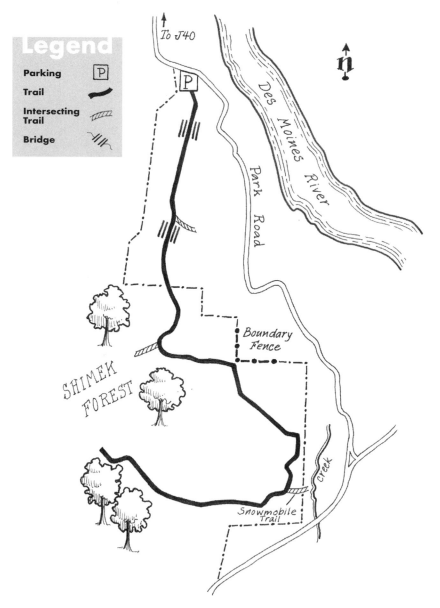

Legend

Parking [P]

Trail

Intersecting Trail

Bridge

To J40

Des Moines River

Park Road

Boundary Fence

SHIMEK FOREST

creek

Snowmobile Trail

any evidence of foot traffic, but the cleared swath through the forest is about 10 to 12 feet wide, so the trail is quite apparent. When you've gone about 1 mile, you'll reach another junction: turn left. (If you turned right, in a few feet you'd reach the end of state land, as marked by a sign.) Notice the shagbark hickory and white oak as you walk along. A boundary line runs near the east side of the path. At a clearing, the trail veers south. Although the path is still covered with vegetation, the general trail remains identifiable because the trees are cleared on each side. If you happen to get caught in the rain, the trail isn't as slick as a dirt path.

Enjoy the gentle, winding downhill at 1.5 miles. Now the path is about 20 feet wide and grassy. Shagbark hickory and white oak are on both sides of your trail. In about 0.25 mile, the forest opens up, and you can actually see sky overhead; the grassy path is still at least 10 feet wide. Look for woodland flowers and other flowers that take advantage of the sunlight in any clearing, no matter how small.

At slightly less than 2 miles into the walk, you'll reach another junction. A snowmobile sign (with an arrow) points to the left. Do not go left. Down this path is a ravine that fills with water after heavy rains, and there is no bridge, so it may not be wise to cross it. Instead, turn right at this junction, onto another grassy, wide trail. Here you'll find several patches of wild bergamot. Stop and listen: you'll hear the rustle of wildlife, birds, and the wind wafting through the forest. But you won't hear traffic or other sounds that permeate daily life. Enjoy!

Continue on this peaceful path for about 0.5 mile (or longer if you wish). You might see a startled doe flick its tail and flee. The path continues on for as far as you can see. (These quiet forest paths can be addictive; be sure to allow enough time to get back to your car before dark.)

When you decide it's time to turn around, simply retrace your steps through the forest, to the park, and then to your car. You haven't made many turns, so you shouldn't run into any difficulties. But the compass or GPS that you packed will come in handy now if you're unsure of the path. You'll notice more snowmobile signs tacked up on trees or posted to the side of the path on the way back. Listen for owls.

Whitebreast Unit Hike
Stephens State Forest

Distance: 6.74 miles

Time: 4 hours

Path: Dirt. These trails are designated for equestrian use, so the path is heavily dimpled where horse hooves have sunk into the wet ground. After a heavy rain, the trail can be quite muddy.

Directions: From U.S. Highway 65 south of Lucas, watch for the State Forest sign and turn west onto 467th Street. Just past the intersection with 130th Avenue you'll see a Whitebreast Unit sign. Continue on; 467th Street becomes 127th Trail as the road curves south. Past the equestrian camp area turn left (east) onto 460th Lane. Park in the day-use parking area for equestrians.

Contact: Stephens State Forest, 1111 North 8th Street, Chariton, IA 50049; (641) 774-4559. www.iowadnr.com/ forestry/stephens

Highlights: This secluded walk takes you into the forest and away from it all. Pay attention to hunting seasons before you go. Although the heavily traveled equestrian areas can be muddy and uneven, it is a pretty walk (especially in the fall). It's quiet here; even the roads are more like a trail. You may not see any other hikers. Take your compass or GPS on this walk, along with water and a backpack.

Start your hike from the day-use parking area and head in a westerly direction on the road. At the fork in the road, turn left (away from the camp) and look across the road: you will see an equestrian trailhead sign. Take this path.

As you begin your walk on this forest path, the trail is only a few feet wide. In the fall, the trail is covered with leaves, such as red oak and shagbark hickory. Watch out for tree roots beneath the leaves on this uneven path. It's a natural path, with branches across the trail too. Deer come bounding through the trees at regular intervals; enjoy their presence. When you've walked about 0.35 mile, you'll reach an intersection. The path to the left leads to the road; go right. The trail widens to about 15 to 20 feet, and it's still covered with leaves. The trail here has had quite a bit of equestrian use; the path is indented with one hoof mark after another. If the path is muddy, stay to the outside of the trail where it's easier to walk. After a heavy rain, it's best to avoid this section of trail—and the muddy mess. (You can pick up the path further down the road.)

At about 0.5 mile, the trail intersects with the road. Walk along the road in a southwesterly direction (about 50 yards). Then pick up the same trail again on your right. Now the path is back to a couple of feet wide, but the mud is gone. Here, you'll be walking on the upper edges of ravines. The terrain is rolling, with gentle uphills and downhills. The winding path continues to meander along the edges of ravines. Notice the large white and red oak trees. If you're hiking in the fall on a windy day, the trees protect you from chilly breezes.

At about 0.75 mile, you'll be at the top of a draw, near the road. This is an access area where vehicles can be parked. To the left, the path leads to the road. Take the wide trail to the right for a short distance. At the fork in the trail, go left. Notice where horses have slid on the trail; it may still be a bit muddy.

At about 1.25 miles the trail intersects with the road again. Look across the road to a bridge. As you cross the bridge, notice the horsetail that has sprung up in this wet area. At the next junction, turn left and begin a steep uphill. After a switchback, you'll be going east for a bit. Notice that the trail has been rerouted in a couple of spots along here; follow the signs. Abundant deer tracks are dwarfed by the multitude of hoof prints in the ground. Soon, you will cross a dried-up creek bed. Now continue uphill on a brief, steep path where you'll see even more deer.

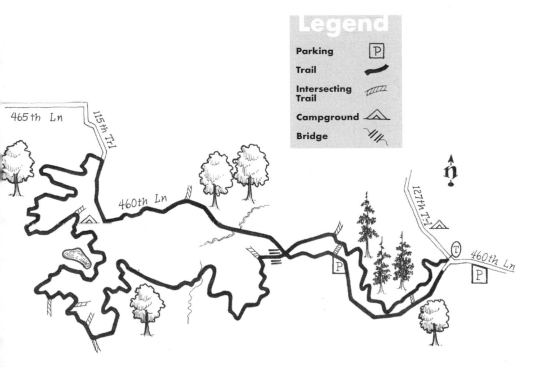

Legend

Parking	P
Trail	
Intersecting Trail	
Campground	
Bridge	

465th Ln

115th Trl

460th Ln

127th Trl

460th Ln

You are still meandering along the top of ravines. When you've walked about 2.5 miles into the forest, stop and take a look around. You're surrounded by tall trees; everywhere you look, you can see the forest. Listen to the forest sounds—and nothing else. Moments like these make the hike worthwhile.

At the next T-intersection, bear right (to the left is a boundary line and a wide path). As you turn, look ahead to where the trail splits again; go left. This seems like a fairly new section of trail, and very few horses have marked this path.

About 3 miles ahead, at the next intersection, turn left. The trail is about 15 to 20 feet wide now—and wet and slick. At the next Y-intersection go right, following the equestrian sign. The path continues to be muddy. At about 3.35 miles, notice the pond below to your left. (You will circle around the pond and end up on the other side.) The path slopes to the left, which makes it difficult to maneuver in the mud. Take your time or you'll end up down in the mud. (A walking stick would help keep you upright through here.) Small white snail shells appear on the path.

At 3.75 miles, take a break on a log across from a camping area just above you. Go straight at the next junction. Now the downhill path is leaf-covered. Notice honey locust here. Continue to tread carefully for the next mile. At almost 5 miles you will intersect with a road. Hooray! To the left, the road is called 465th Lane. To the right, it is called 115th Trail.

Turn right on this dirt-lane road. You'll appreciate the level surface of the road. Take this road as you head back. (It's easy to pick up the path again if you wish.) But the dirt road is just as quiet and secluded as the trail. Soon you'll pass by the camp you saw from below. After this camping area, the road changes to gravel.

The road now intersects with 460th Lane; follow 460th Lane to the left. You are still on top of the ridge as you walk the road. Continue to walk the road on a downhill stretch. Soon, the road crosses over a creek (at about 6 miles into the walk). Look to the right side of the road at a large stand of pine on a hillside. You'll continue to see rows and rows of pine for the next 0.5 mile or so. What a pleasant way to end this hike!

Next, you'll reach the intersection of 127th Trail and 460th Lane. Head to the day-use parking area, clean the mud off your shoes, and go home. But the forest is addictive; you'll be back.

Hills to Valleys

Hitchcock Nature Center

Badger Ridge Walk
Hitchcock Nature Center

Distance: .65 mile

Time: 50 minutes

Path: Dirt path, grass.

Directions: From Council Bluffs, take Interstate 29 north to Exit 61A (Crescent/Hitchcock Nature Center), which takes you to County Road G37. When you reach the T-intersection at Crescent, turn left (north) onto County Road L20 (also called the Old Lincoln Highway). You're now on the Loess Hills Scenic Byway. In about 5 miles, turn left onto Page Lane; a sign points the way to Hitchcock Nature Center. Turn right onto Ski Hill Loop. This goes directly into Hitchcock Nature Center. Check the signboard and information at the entrance (and pay a $2 per vehicle fee). Follow the park road toward the lodge; park near the Badger Ridge trailhead.

Contact: Hitchcock Nature Center, Pottawattamie County Conservation, 27792 Ski Hill Loop, Honey Creek, IA 51542; (712) 545-3283. www.pottcounty.com

Highlights: Overlooks, ridges, and prairie—and a beautiful view of the hills on the lodge's observation deck. Check out the Hawkwatch stats posted here. During fall migration watch for hawks from the deck, where thousands of hawks have been spotted and recorded by volunteers.

Begin your walk at the Badger Ridge Access trailhead. Across the road from the trailhead is a kiosk and brochures (with a map). Before or after your walk, head to the observation deck at the lodge (just past this trailhead). Gaze at the rumpled Loess Hills spread out before you. This is a great place to bird-watch. (Use the scope if you wish.) Notice the Hawkwatch stats posted here. Hawks you might see include Swainson's, red-tailed, broad-winged, and sharp-shinned hawks. Look at the impressive Hawkwatch counts: thousands of hawks have been observed and documented here.

Return to the trailhead and begin your walk with a descent. The dirt trail is about four feet across and washed out in the middle. Several boards have been placed to help with erosion. The descent becomes steeper and the trail widens to about five feet. Notice the red cedar and the light-colored loess soil. Look for wild raspberries in season and pale purple coneflower.

Now you're on a ridge; on either side of the path is a ravine. You'll spot more red cedar and some oak too. Soon you'll be at a photo op point with a clear view. (You can see Interstate 29 from here.) Admire the hills.

The path now consists of two dirt ruts with grass between. Look for wild grape along here. Follow the path; enjoy the purple prairie clover and leadplant, along with other prairie plants. Watch for the race runner along here, an interesting little lizard that is fun to spot (not the same as the prairie skink).

At about 0.5 mile, you'll have had several opportunities to get an eyeful. Gaze out over planted fields and the Loess Hills. A bench is provided so you can sit and gawk for a while. Here, you have a good view of the cone-shaped tips of the hills, their gentle shapes. Walk along and enjoy the view. In summer, notice that plenty of leadplants are in bloom. Purple prairie clover dots the landscape in early summer; pale purple coneflowers peak later. After the overlook, the path wanders up and down a bit; and you get a feel for walking on the hills. This walk is popular, according to the ranger, because you're able to hike through prairie, the hills, and timber.

Now you'll come to a sign and a fork in the path. Continue on Badger Ridge, past the Hidden Valley junction to the right. This section is mostly downhill.

At about 0.75 mile, you will be at a primitive campsite. There isn't much to see here, but it is your turnaround point. Retrace your steps along the ridge and enjoy the vistas again.

Ready for More?

Make this a loop and turn right onto the Hidden Valley Trail (instead of descending to the campsite). Keep making right-hand turns to get back to the parking area.

Legend

Parking	P
Trail	
Intersecting Trail	
View	
Campsite	

Overlook Hike
Hitchcock Nature Center

Distance: 3.62 miles

Time: 2.5 hours

Path: Dirt path, grass. The well-marked paths keep you on track. According to the map provided in Hitchcock's brochure, the trails along this walk are considered moderate to difficult.

Directions: See directions for Walk 9.

Contact: Hitchcock Nature Center, Pottawattamie County Conservation, 27792 Ski Hill Loop, Honey Creek, IA 51542; (712) 545-3283. www.pottcounty.com

Highlights: Wonderful lookouts on top of ridges. You can see Omaha from several vantage points. The paths are steep in many places, but the views and vistas make it worthwhile.

Begin your walk at the kiosk, located at the trailhead for Fox Run Ridge. Stuff a brochure/map into your pack or pocket: the map's colored-coded trails are marked according to the level of difficulty. (The trails on this walk are described as moderate to difficult.)

The wood-chip trail begins near the kiosk (to the right as you face it). At the first junction turn left and head for the "Chute." This is a steep downhill path with high banks on each side. The Chute is aptly named. It's a popular spot for tubing in the winter—and as you walk along you can understand why! The banks are high and the path curves and turns. Imagine sliding down this trail, banking the corners like a bobsled run. Fun! The return climb would be a task though.

As you near the end of the Chute, bear left at a junction. Now you're on Bluestem Meander Trail. Notice the wild grape along here in the summer. Continue on the steep downhill trail for a while longer. Soon the path turns grassy and opens up into a small clearing dotted with black-eyed Susans. Now you'll enter deep woods on a dirt trail, about six to eight feet wide. Here, the path levels off somewhat. At the next intersection, you'll leave Bluestem Meander and continue on the Hidden Valley Trail, which extends to the left and right. Turn right.

Notice the ferns on your walk. Maidenhair fern grows in a circular fashion, easy to spot. To your right is a ravine; on your left is a hillside. About 0.5 mile into the walk, your path veers left. Now you're walking among tall trees. You'll see black walnut here.

At about 0.75 mile, turn right; now you're on Westridge Trail (Hidden Valley Trail continues left). Here, thick grass covers the path whenever there is an opening in the woods. A couple of dirt ruts have been worn in the wide grassy path. If the grass is high, you won't notice the vines and might trip, so watch your step.

At about 1 mile, you'll start a steep climb. Wooden blocks with rubber "treads" have been placed on the trail at intervals to discourage erosion. This steep incline stretches on for 0.5 mile—and you'll definitely feel it. (You've climbed about 175 vertical feet in this distance.) Now you are near the top of the ridge. Notice the terrestrial snails along the path. These land snails are fun to spot.

You'll see oak along here. Of course, now that you're on the ridge, there are ravines on both sides, but you haven't been rewarded with any spectacular views—yet. Be patient, the vistas are just ahead. Now you'll have a bit of a downhill; watch the vines on the path again. At the next junction, turn right.

Just when you think you couldn't possibly climb any higher—you will. (Now you know why the brochure labels this section of trail difficult; the challenge is in the steep ascents and descents.) You'll climb another 100 feet before you reach the overlook.

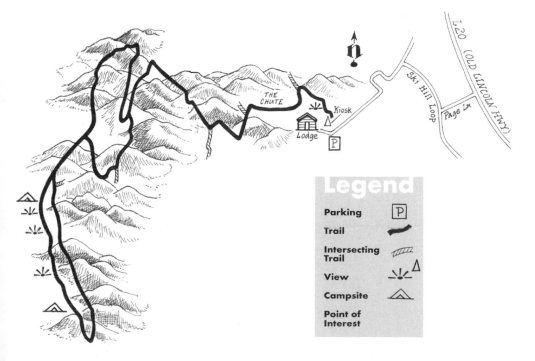

Scramble up the steep Westridge trail at Hitchcock Nature Center for spectacular vistas.

At 1.5 miles, you'll reach a junction that marks a loop. The sign lets you know that Westridge Trail loops here. Continue straight. Now you'll pass a campsite to the right. Step off the path and check out the view here. The climb is beginning to pay off. Vegetation on the path holds back your pace as you maneuver around vines. If you brought your walking stick on this walk, good for you!

Just past the primitive campsite (1.5 miles into the walk) is a nice overlook. You can see downtown Omaha from here. Continue on. The next vista is even better. Now you've hiked almost 2 miles; you've reached the highest point of the walk. Enjoy! Look out over fields, the Loess Hills, Omaha in the distance. You are high above the treetops. Yup. The climb was worth it.

This is another primitive campsite. It wouldn't be easy to carry a tent up here, but what a place to camp! Spend some time at the top of the ridge. (Bring out the energy bars and water.) When you're through gawking at the views, continue on the same path, which loops around on the backside of the ridge. You'll have the same steep ups-and-downs, of course, but you know what to expect now.

When you reach the loop junction, bear right and retrace your steps along the Westridge Trail for a short distance. At the next junction, turn right. This is called the Shortcut Trail on Hitchcock's map. The Shortcut will lead you to the Hidden Valley Trail.

Navigate another steep downhill, then enter a canopy of trees. The path is once again two ruts with vegetation in the middle. As you descend, look for woodland flowers, including the purple and blue blooms of the tall bellflower. Notice the honey locust trees too. You're in a low area now; ridges rise on both sides of the path.

At about 2.75 miles, bear left at a junction. Now you are back on Hidden Valley Trail. Almost immediately you'll reach another junction. Veer right and stay on Hidden Valley Trail (to the left is Westridge Trail.) Now retrace your steps to the trailhead and parking.

Ready for More?

Choose another trail at Hitchcock Nature Center. How about Fox Run Ridge to Dozer Cut?

Ridge and Bridge Walk
Waubonsie State Park

Distance: 3 miles

Time: 1.5 hours

Path: Dirt, grass. You'll walk among tall trees, into a valley, and along a ridge. The wooded paths are well marked.

Directions: From Council Bluffs, go about 40 miles on Interstate 29 to Exit 10; leave the interstate and go east on State Highway 2 for about 5 miles. Turn south on County Road L48 (also Waubonsie Park Road), which will take you into the park. Follow the signs that direct you to the overlook shelter and parking area. (The park office is near the parking area.)

Contact: Waubonsie State Park, 2585 Waubonsie Park Road, Hamburg, IA 51640; (712) 382-2786. www.iowadnr.com/parks

Highlights: A great hike in the Loess Hills. Walk into a valley and up on a ridge. The views are wonderful on the ridge. Be sure to take a look at the unusual loess soil. As glaciers melted and receded in Iowa, the loess (silt) was picked up by the wind and redistributed, creating the lovely Loess Hills. (These deposits are found only in Iowa, Missouri, and China.)

Begin your walk in the parking area near the map board and several trailheads. Bridge Trail and Valley Trail head off to the right, which is the way you will go. The shaded path is about six feet across. There is a ravine on the right, and a ridge on the left. Although the path isn't steep yet, it promises to be. At the first junction, a sign alerts you that Bridge Trail is straight ahead. Keep going. Do not turn right.

The winding, curvy trail gets steeper; now you can see exposed tree roots on the ridge on the left (a ravine is still to the right). Notice the light-colored, loose loess soil as you walk. In a few minutes, at a T-intersection, turn right (the path is signed for other trails as well). Bear right and continue on; you're walking on the top of a ridge. Notice the bur oaks along here. The huge trees have unusual bends and twists; keep an eye on them!

When you've gone about 0.5 mile, continue straight at a junction. Note the signs here because you will take the other path on the way back. (The Bridge Trail is about 0.35 mile straight ahead.) Now the path is about three feet wide and you'll start to descend again. Look at the huge hollow oak tree that is still standing! It looks more like a statue than a tree.

At about 1 mile, at a fork in the path, go straight (do not turn right). Now the path levels off, after descending more than 125 feet. Past this intersection is a bridge. At this point, you can hear traffic because you are nearing State Highway 2. Look down the 49 steep steps to the wooden bridge. This is the lowest spot of the walk. The wooden bridge is about 45 feet long. After the bridge, the path leads up a short incline to State Highway 2. This is your turnaround point.

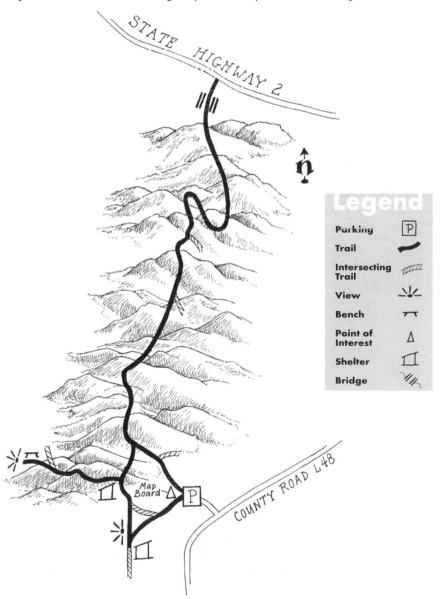

Legend

Parking	P
Trail	➤
Intersecting Trail	⬚
View	☀
Bench	⊓
Point of Interest	△
Shelter	⌂
Bridge	⫽

Waubonsie State Park features some steep climbs and descents.

Retrace your steps past the Valley Trail intersection. Keep climbing! Turn right at the next junction, and continue going up. At the next Y-intersection, take a right to Ridge Trail. As you come around a bend, you anticipate some nice scenery—and you will have just that! You are looking out across the treetops! You've walked 2.25 miles to this point. The three-foot-wide trail is on the edge of a ridge. And, of course, you're still ascending.

In less than 0.25 mile, you'll be at the highest point of your walk. As you walk along the treetops, you'll reach a bench and a vista. Sit on the bench; your feet literally dangle over the edge of the ridge. Wow. It doesn't get any better than this. Take some time to soak up the beauty of the Loess Hills.

This is your turnaround point. (The trail continues on, but it eventually dead-ends.) Enjoy the views as you walk the narrow ridge back to the last trail junction; bear right. You'll reach a circular stone shelter that is quite unique. Walk past a bench on the left; you can see the ridge you just walked on. From the shelter, head for the Overlook Trail, which is a popular spot. Lots of visitors walk to the Overlook and don't hike any other trails. Enjoy another vista; read the signboards about the Loess Hills. When you're through, return to the map board and signs—and your car.

Vista to Valley Hike
Waubonsie State Park

Distance: 4 miles

Time: 2 hours or longer

Path: Dirt, crushed rock, grass. You'll walk on top of ridges and down into valleys. The paths narrow and widen and may be washed out in a few spots, but they're always well marked.

Directions: See directions for Walk 11.

Contact: Waubonsie State Park, 2585 Waubonsie Park Road, Hamburg, IA 51640; (712) 382-2786. www.iowadnr.com/parks

Highlights: With its steep ridges and scenic overlooks, traipsing through the Loess Hills is hiking at its best. These hills are addictive; you'll want to return again and again.

    The Loess Hills' unique landscape formed as glaciers melted and receded. The remaining loess (silt) was carried by the wind and redistributed. You'll find such unusual deposits of loess only in Iowa, Missouri, and China.

The trailhead and map board are visible from the parking area. At the map board, pick up a park brochure/trail map. Read about the Loess Hills too. Waubonsie, for example, was named for a Pottawattamie chief. Several of the park's signboards mention Lewis and Clark; this park is on the Lewis and Clark Historic Trail. Imagine seeing the hills through these explorers' eyes.

Follow the short trail to your left that heads toward Sunset Ridge Trail. You'll make another left turn almost immediately and pass by a shelter house. Straight ahead, you can see Sunset Ridge Trail—take it. The crushed-rock/dirt trail is about eight feet wide at this point. As you walk the shady path, notice the ironwood, large oak, and some pine.

About 0.5 mile into your walk, the trail meets with a road. Don't cross the road. Stay on the path as it curves to the right (still on Sunset Ridge). You're out of the woods now, in a clearing. The area to the left has been designated as prairie restoration: The wildflower display includes plenty of coneflowers. In summer months, look for monarchs and other butterflies flitting nearby.

After the prairie, head back into the woods (at about 1.35 miles). Note the steep ravines on both sides of the trail. In about 0.5 mile, you'll come to another pleasant patch of prairie. Then it's downhill. A slanting ravine is on the left, at the path's edge. To the right, tree roots

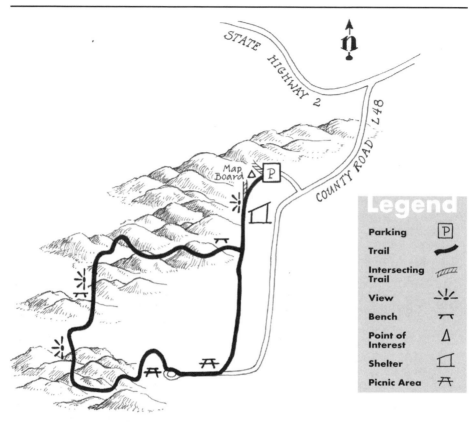

are exposed on the steep slope. Look down into the ravine and across the hills. The hills fold into one another—a beautiful sight. The gently curved, rounded hollows are shaped like a bowl. In the distance, deer shake their tails and disappear.

At 2 miles, you'll come up an incline. Shortly after this—what a view! A bench faces a fantastic overlook. Here, look across to three other states: Kansas, Missouri, and Nebraska! Stay and gawk awhile—this will likely be your favorite spot of the entire hike—or any hike. The breathtaking view from this ridgetop showcases the Loess Hills in all its splendor. Look at the texture of the farmers' fields. Notice where the croplands cease and the ridges rise, and how the turkey vultures turn and dip high in the sky—yet they're below you.

The signboard here has information about the Loess Hills. At this point, you've ascended about 329 feet. Behind the bench, look at the geological mark embedded in the path, a metal piece marked U.S. Coast and Geodetic Survey. Look closely at the ground—you might see some skinks darting around. Yucca plants grow here too. The wide trail you've been walking ceases near the overlook (the official end to Sunset Ridge Trail), but a narrow, foot-wide dirt trail takes its place.

At about 2.25 miles, you're at an unmarked lookout point. Nice!

Take a good look before you continue—the trail bends back to the left. The downhill path is a deep, narrow groove that has washed out. As you walk, notice some ironwood along here. Eventually, trees start to overhang the trail again. The light-colored loess soil is powdery and loose, so pay attention to your footing.

At 2.5 miles, you'll head uphill again. It's an incredible feeling to walk on the top of these hills. Stop often and look around—you're still above the treetops! The grassy ridges plunge down to farmers' fields. Note the wild grape and red oak to the left. Then, as you descend, the path again washes out and becomes another deep groove in the ground, about a foot deep. Soon you'll see red cedar on both sides of the path.

From an overlook in Waubonsie State Park, visitors can gaze beyond hills and fields to Kansas, Missouri, and Nebraska.

The path is like a roller coaster; now you'll head back up. Here, notice a mix of trees: cottonwood, red cedar, and red oak. Then you'll start another steep descent. Take it slowly—it's a toes-crunched-against-the-front-of-your-boots kind of downhill. Tree roots in the trail create natural footholds, so take advantage of them. Grab hold of a tree branch hanging over the path if you need to—it's that steep. A log on the side of the trail provides a pleasant place for a quick break.

Part of Waubonsie's charm is its seclusion. You probably won't meet any hikers on the longer trails. But wildlife is all around. Watch for the flash of red of the scarlet tanager. You may even spot a broad-winged hawk. At about 2.65 miles, you'll see a crumbling stone structure—and the doorway from what was likely a root cellar on an old farmstead. Feel the cool air seeping out as you walk by. You're at the bottom of the ridge (in the valley that you looked down upon earlier), having descended about 219 feet from the overlook area.

Now it's time to go back up—and, of course, it's just as steep. The trail widens a bit, though, to about three feet wide. As you leave the woods and enter an open area, a whole slew of wild raspberries (in summer) awaits. Look for hoary vervain too—the spikes of purple add color to the landscape. At the top of this hill the path intersects with a road. (You could park here and hike to the overlooks too. Just follow the park road to this spot.) You've walked about 3 miles to this point.

On your right is a parking area with a picnic table and grill. A turn-around is straight ahead, and a road is to your left. Walk toward the picnic and restroom area through the turnaround. The area is well marked with signs, so you won't have any trouble picking up the trail. Just past the picnic area, on the left side, is the trailhead sign. This section of the trail is part of the Mincer Nature Trail. Signboards provide information about the prairie and identify several of the grasses, such as big bluestem and Indian grass. After the prairie, you'll enter a wooded area with oak, red cedar, and some brushy shrubs.

At 3.35 miles, you're heading north, parallel to the road on your right. The grass path changes to dirt. Soon the path comes out of the woods, near the road. Go past the red water pump. Continue straight (north)—the trail picks up again in just a few hundred feet.

At about 3.5 miles, you're back at the Sunset Ridge junction you took on the way out. Continue straight, past the shelter house to the Overlook Trail junction. Then take this short trail left, up the 21 railroad-tie steps to the overlook. Although this vista doesn't pack the same punch as the Sunset Ridge Overlook, it's still a great way to end your walk. The signboard calls the Loess Hills "an American treasure." After this 4-mile hike across ridges and through valleys, you'll surely agree.

Follow the path back to the map board and the parking area to end your walk. Before you leave, grab a pawpaw fruit from the trees by the parking lot and enjoy!

Ready for More?
The Picnic Area Trail is worth a look too. Late summer and early fall, about 50 pawpaw trees bear ripe fruit. The fruit has an unusual, mango-type flavor.

Historic Sites and Timeless Treks

Preparation Canyon State Park

Boneyard Hollow Hike
Dolliver Memorial State Park

Distance: 3 miles

Time: 3.5 hours

Path: Crushed rock, natural rock, grass, dirt. On several steep sections you're simply walking along rock outcroppings.

Directions: From Harcourt, travel north on U.S. Highway 169. Turn right (east) on County Road D43. Watch for the Dolliver Memorial sign directing you to the state park. Turn left at Dolliver Park Avenue. The hard-surface road winds down into the park. Continue past the sign for the Group Camp and South Lodge to a map board and kiosk where you can stop and pick up a brochure/map. The Copperas Beds trailhead sign is a short distance down the road. Pull into the parking area across the road from the trailhead.

Contact: Dolliver Memorial State Park, 2757 Dolliver Park Avenue, Lehigh, IA 50557; (515) 359-2539. www.iowadnr.com/parks

Highlights: Walk past Copperas Beds, Indian Mounds, and Boneyard Hollow. Enjoy an abundance of red-headed woodpeckers. The history of this quiet, peaceful park makes the walk even more interesting.

Begin your walk at the Copperas Beds trailhead. The four-foot-wide crushed-rock path is covered with oak leaves in the fall. In late autumn, with bare trees, it's easy to spot the multitude of red-headed woodpeckers in the area. Head west past a large sandstone boulder at the trailhead.

The path soon drifts into a 50-foot-wide grassy area—and the trail picks up on the far side. Note the big walnut tree in the clearing. Now the trail is simply dirt. Just ahead is a junction with a sign that points out the Copperas Beds to the left. Turn left and climb about 29 steps to an overlook. Check out the Copperas Beds, the sandstone formations that rise more than 90 feet above Prairie Creek. Notice the colors on the rock face: orange, green, rose, and white. Mineral deposits on the sandstone account for some of the color. Unfortunately, you'll find initials carved into the sandstone as well.

Then return to the trail and cross the creek on a wooden plank bridge. Here, the horsetail is as thick as grass; it covers the forest floor for about 50 feet on either side of the path. At the next junction turn right; follow the sign with the hiker symbol.

After you've climbed more than 120 stone steps (each step fash-

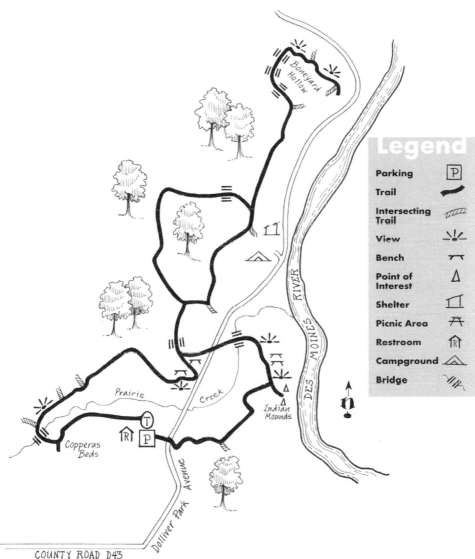

Parking ▣

Trail

Intersecting Trail

View

Bench

Point of Interest △

Shelter ⊓

Picnic Area

Restroom ⌂R⌂

Campground △

Bridge

Boneyard Hollow

DES MOINES RIVER

Prairie Creek

Indian Mounds

Copperas Beds

Dolliver Park Avenue

COUNTY ROAD D43

ioned from three stones placed together), you'll be at a lookout point —a nice vista. Look down more than 55 feet to the creek below, then climb about 20 railroad-tie steps to the top of the bluff. Don't take the trail to the left; continue to walk along the bluff's edge. Be cautious if the widely placed stairs are covered with leaves; the path is about one step from the edge. Watch for tree roots too.

Enjoy the peace and quiet; listen to the birds and the wind as you navigate around a few big boulders and fieldstones in the path. Late autumn, the leaves are about six inches deep on the trail, obscuring the narrow path. Crunching through the thick layer of leaves is sure to startle deer into taking flight. As you walk, the steep drop-off to the right becomes a more gradual slope.

When you've walked about 0.5 mile, you'll come to another junction. Bear right; continue along the bluff's edge through woods. Note the shagbark hickory trees. The path levels out for a while, then it's back to a gentle up and down. A barbed-wire fence marks a boundary of the park at about 0.75 mile. Enjoy the showy red-headed woodpeckers, perhaps dozens of them. At the next vista, pay attention to the sign that says No Hiking (down the cliff). It's a reminder that this spot is a lookout only—not a way down the steep slope.

After this vista, the path descends. Trees hug the three-foot-wide path. As you descend from the top of the cliff and wind down, notice the natural rock on the path. At about 1 mile into your walk, a pair of wooden benches marks the next junction, which is a switchback. This is a wonderful spot to watch the red-headed woodpeckers. Go left on the switchback (the only other path leads down to the road). Now hike across a moss-covered stone bridge that goes through a wash. You've descended about 100 vertical feet from your vista on the cliff. Woodpeckers continue to flit by as you start a long, winding climb on a narrow dirt trail. Maple and cottonwood are noticeable in this low area.

Now veer to the left at a Y-intersection. The understory trees are more noticeable along with many deer; it's not uncommon to see about 10 or more at a time—including some big bucks. Around a curve, notice the cornfield and boundary line to the left—and more deer. The path levels out just before a stand of aspen. In the fall, aspen leaves cover the path.

At about 1.5 miles, the ravine on the right becomes fairly steep again. The path is near the edge—not a place where you'd want to take a tumble. Now you'll descend again. Watch for numerous rocks and boulders in the path. Here, it's one rock after another or one boulder after another. As you approach a bridge, be sure you have firm footing on the uneven stone steps beneath the thick layer of leaves. The descent to the bridge is steep and difficult. Trekking poles or a walking stick would come in handy here. You've walked about 1.75 miles to this point. The wooden plank bridge is about 30 feet long. You are down in a hollow with ridges on both sides.

At the next intersection, bear left on your way to Boneyard Hollow. Now you're ascending on a long, gradual incline. And you'll still see an amazing number of red-headed woodpeckers. Continue straight at the next junction. Cross a stone bridge at about 2 miles. After you cross it, turn around and look—from this vantage point you can tell that it is a stone arch bridge. Anytime you stop, you'll see woodpeckers. The wooded path is quiet and serene. As the path becomes steeper, you'll come to another moss-covered stone bridge. It's over a draw, with no water at this time. As you continue on, you're walking on a tight pathway between rocks.

Now you have a great view of Boneyard Hollow! Look at the narrow ravine between the rock walls. Cross another bridge and begin another uphill climb. Here, you're just making your way around rocks and outcroppings. Continue straight at the next junction. (Turning left will take you to a picnic area with a restroom.) Keep going and take the path as it descends to the road, so you can check out the rest of Boneyard Hollow. This is a gradual decline with about 50 stone and railroad-tie steps.

Down at the road, look into the mouth of Boneyard Hollow. It is said that the name "Boneyard Hollow" was given because of the large number of buffalo bones found in the canyon. Envision buffalo grazing here in the past, at that time herded into the narrow ravine.

Now retrace your steps past Boneyard Hollow until you reach the junction that also leads to the lodge. Bear left; take the uphill path to the lodge. A sign at the top of the hill points the way to the lodge or a trail to the right. Take the trail to the right.

You have an uphill climb ahead. Stay on the trail that curves right at the next junction (the trail to the left heads down a ravine). When you reach the next intersection, you've completed a loop; you're back on a section of trail that you took on the way out to Boneyard Hollow. Go straight. Now enjoy a long, gradual downhill. You've walked about 4 miles to this point.

At the next junction, turn left toward a parking area, playground, and a road. (You haven't been on this trail before.) Head east across the parking area; you can see the trailhead and a bridge across the road. The 60-foot-long bridge feels spongy as you walk across it. Now you'll climb again. After about 100 steps (you've hiked about 4.25 miles to this point), enjoy a break and several vistas (benches are provided). Take a short detour to view the Indian mounds just ahead if you wish. Then return to the main trail and follow the bluff.

Continue on the main trail that curves to the right at the next junction. As you descend, thick leaves obscure your path here, too, so watch your step. The path intersects with the park road; follow it back to your car. You'll exit the trail near the Group Camp sign you saw on the way into the park.

Canyon and Prairie Hike
Preparation Canyon State Park

Distance: 4 miles

Time: 2.8 hours

Path: Dirt, mowed grass, and prairie. Be prepared for sharp inclines and steep descents through woods and prairie, on top of a ridge, and into a valley. Other than the trailhead and campsites, the trails are unmarked.

Directions: Travel on State Highway 183 south of Moorhead for several miles. Turn right (west) onto 314th Street. Follow this road to the park, where you can't miss the huge park sign! You'll see a signboard and overlook almost immediately. Take a look at the gorgeous view and continue on, until you reach a board with park information and brochures/maps. Turn left here onto a small loop that serves as a parking area near the trailhead.

Contact: c/o Lewis and Clark State Park, 21914 Park Loop, Onawa, IA 51040; (712) 423-2829. www.iowadnr.com/parks

Highlights: Although the trails have some of the steepest inclines you'll find on these hikes, you'll also be rewarded with great vistas. Walk through native prairie and bur oak forest. You'll descend into a canyon and climb to the top of a ridge. The seclusion and untouched beauty of this park add to its appeal; you truly feel away from it all.

The area's history is as colorful as the landscape. Mormons settled in the Loess Hills in the 1800s after leaving the wagon train to Utah. This valley was to be their "School of Preparation for the Life Beyond." A few years later many Mormons left, parting ways with their leader who became rich off the land—at their expense. Although the town of Preparation doesn't exist today, the scenic valley is much the same as when the Mormons arrived by covered wagons.

Begin your hike at the trailhead, noticeable from the parking area. The wooded, dirt path is about four feet wide. In just a few hundred feet, you'll be at the first trail juncture: turn right. (There is another trail marker to guide you.) The path changes to grass after the turn and you'll start to descend into the canyon. The landscape alternates between ridges and ravines along the trails, up and down through the park.

As the trail curves to the left, you'll see some basswood along with bur oak. If you need a break, a bench is available here. To the left is a ravine; tree roots are exposed on the sloping hillside on the right.

You'll hike several switchbacks here, still descending into the canyon. (The ravine is on your right for a while as you head east.) Look for maidenhair fern along the path. (It grows in a curved half-circle, an unusual shape!) Notice the moss on the trail at times.

Just 0.35 mile into the walk, you've already descended about 200 feet into a canyon. The air is still. Quiet surrounds you, interrupted occasionally by a few birds' voices, some sweet, some insistent—and the muffled scrunch of your own footsteps. What you won't hear is traffic of any kind. You might pass by a couple of hikers in the canyon or no one at all. Camping at this park is hike-in only; the trails pass by several of these campsites.

When you've walked almost 1 mile, you'll reach another junction; turn left. (Right will take you down to a picnic area with a restroom and drinking water spigot.) If you decide to fill up your water bottles and take this detour, just retrace your steps (about 0.35 mile total) back to the junction when you're done. At this junction, notice the

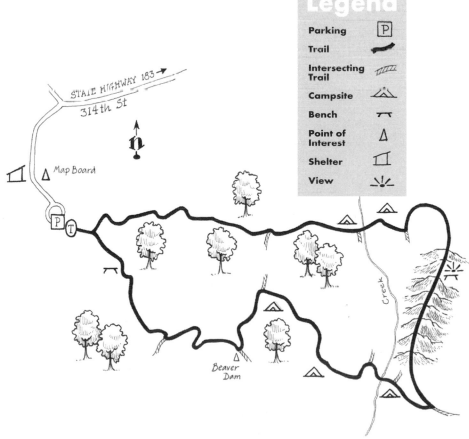

Hikers can traipse along a prairie ridge at Preparation Canyon State Park.

deep ruts and the mounded earth in front of you. Imagine stage-coaches bouncing down the hill, their wheels creaking and settling into the ruts, one after another.

Take several switchbacks through the canyon now. Just before the beaver dams, turn left. But before you do, check out the dams. Frogs and other wetland inhabitants blend so well into their environment that it takes a minute or two to realize they're around—lots of them. If the beavers aren't visible, their handiwork will be. Jewelweed has sprung up along the path.

Now go back and make your left turn. This path marks one of the steepest ascents in the park (even with a couple of switchbacks). You're still climbing at the next junction. Take the path to the right, past hike-in campsite #8. (In about 0.1 mile, you've climbed 183 feet.)

Notice the red cedar along the path. A barbed-wire fence to the right marks a boundary. Now the trail begins a steep descent. In the fall, leaves cover the path—hiding fruits and twigs—so it's easy to slip on the loose loess soil. At about 1.65 miles, you'll reach campsite #7. At almost 2 miles, bear right at a junction and then cross a small creek. After you cross the creek, the prairie ridge comes into view. Turn right and pass by campsite #1.

In less than 0.25 mile, turn left at a junction. This takes you onto the prairie ridge—where you'll begin an ascent. Big bluestem, probably taller than you, waves in the wind on this wide, mowed prairie path. Look out across farmers' fields. At about 2.5 miles, stop at the bench and let your gaze skim the treetops. What a great place to view autumn's collage of color!

On the way down the prairie ridge, notice the bur oak at about 2.65 miles. At the next junction, bear right. Sumac accents your path with streaks of scarlet in late summer and fall. The trail meanders in and out of woods and across some patches of prairie. Goldenrod crowns the prairie in September.

At almost 3 miles, the path veers slightly left—stay on it. (To the right is campsite #4.) Soon after this, cross the creek again. Then turn right, past campsite #5, and stay in the woods for the remainder of your walk. At the next junction, go straight. You'll see ridges on both sides of you now—you're still fairly low. As you climb uphill, the woods become denser and the trees increase in size. A barbed-wire fence is on the right as you wind up the path. As soon as you master this incline, you'll head back down—and then back up again. Whew. Although you're close to the end of the hike and more than ready for a level path, you still have one short-but-steep incline to take care of. (Don't groan.)

Now you can see the parking area where you began this walk. Go straight at the next junction. In about 20 feet turn right, and you're at the trailhead. If you didn't spot any wild turkeys on the walk, watch for them on your way out of the park.

Ready for More?

Pick another spot in the lovely Loess Hills to explore. Visit Preparation Cemetery, established in the 1860s by the Mormons.

Fossil, Kiln, and River Trails
Fossil and Prairie Park

Distance: 2.52 miles

Time: 1 hour

Path: Crushed rock, gravel.

Directions: From West Main Avenue in Rockford, turn left onto SW 8th Street (a sign says the park is 1 mile away). SW 8th Street is now County Road T18. At the intersection with County Road B47, turn west on B47 (also called 215th Street). You will see a sign for the Fossil and Prairie Park before you make a right turn into the driveway. Park near the picnic shelter.

Contact: Floyd County Conservation Board, 1227 215th Street, P.O. Box 495, Rockford, IA 50468; (641) 756-3490. www.floydcoia.org

Highlights: Walk along the fossil quarry with a view down into the pits. See historic kilns as you follow the trail to the town of Rockford. Then stop at the quarry and search for Devonian fossils before you leave! These fossils are more than 350 million years old.

Begin your walk at the signboard near the picnic shelter. A gravel trail leads you to the first intersection; the prairie is to the left, the fossil and kiln trails (and the river) are straight ahead. Continue straight. As you walk across a clearing, look ahead to the split-rail fence that marks the trailhead. To the right, notice the various ponds and the water-filled quarry.

The five-foot-wide crushed-rock path heads downhill. The pits are on both sides as you navigate this portion of the path. Railroad-tie steps, about six feet apart, help with the erosion—and your footing. Basically, you are walking on gravel mounds in the pits.

At about 0.2 mile, you'll begin to leave this part of the quarry behind. Notice the crushed-brick and clay tiles that give the path a reddish hue. Large cottonwood trees sprawl along the path too. Several trails veer off to the pits; stay on the main trail. At slightly less than 0.5 mile, you'll pass by the historic kilns on your left (used for brick and tile products as early as the 1890s).

As you continue on, notice a few spur trails that lead to the quarry. Ignore them. Stay on the same path. When you reach a farmer's field, veer right and continue on. You'll see quite a bit of cottonwood along here, too, as well as Virginia waterleaf and wild roses. At about 0.75 mile, cross the Winnebago River on a long bridge.

Now crushed rock thins out, and you'll walk some grassy patches. Listen to the frogs—and pheasants too. The land is rather marshy on both sides of the trail. You might see some spiderwort. Notice the barbed-wire fence on the right. As you get closer to town, you will see the grain elevator. At about 1.25 miles, you'll reach a wooded area (and a house on your right). Pass through a red gate at the end of the trail; you're in Rockford! West Main Avenue and 9th Street intersect slightly to the right of the trail. A sign and bench wait near the road. (The sign identifies the trail.) After a quick break on the bench, retrace your steps to the picnic shelter.

Walk down to the quarry before you leave and search for fossils. You'll find several within minutes! The signboard near the picnic area fills you in on the history of the fossil beds and the types of fossils you might find. (Iowa was once covered by an ocean.) Brachiopods are the most common fossils found here. You might find crinoids or coral as well. (The Fossil and Prairie Center, near the prairie trails, has tons of information and exhibits.) Fill your pockets, or take home one or two, it's your choice.

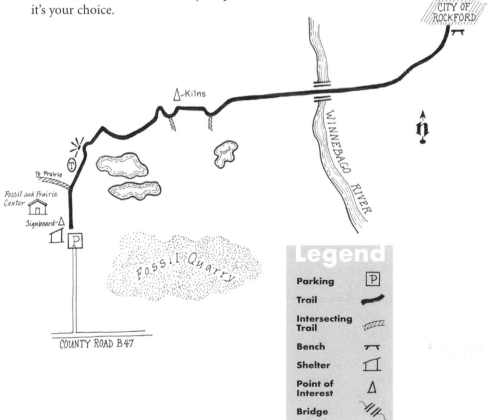

Lacey-Keosauqua Trails
Lacey-Keosauqua State Park

Distance: 5.77 miles

Time: 3 hours

Path: Dirt, grass, remnants of crushed rock. The up-and-down trails are pleasant. As you near the Keosauqua Bridge, you'll encounter several switchbacks and some steep inclines. You are, after all, hiking valleys and bluffs along the Des Moines River. Take your walking stick, if you wish. You'll cross several bridges along the way.

Directions: Southbound on State Highway 1 through Keosauqua, turn right into the park entrance as soon as you cross the bridge over the Des Moines River. Northbound travelers on State Highway 1 will turn left just before the bridge. Follow the park road several miles toward the lodge (watch signs), past the shelter house, picnic area, and the Ely Ford Mormon Crossing. When you reach the lodge, park in front of it. Trail access is directly behind the lodge.

Contact: Lacey-Keosauqua State Park, P.O. Box 398, Keosauqua, IA 52565; (319) 293-3502. www.iowadnr.com/parks

Highlights: Stroll through history as you walk the wooded trails past Indian mounds and to the site known as the Ely Ford Mormon Crossing (part of the Mormon Pioneer Trail). Here, Mormons crossed the Des Moines River as they traveled west through Iowa. Watch for wild turkey on this walk.

Begin your walk at the trailhead access behind the lodge. As you walk along the five-foot-wide dirt trail, you'll find oak leaves, small fallen branches, and even some moss—a typical path through woods. Nineteen Indian mounds are located along this first part of your walk, until you reach the Ely Ford Mormon Crossing. But the mounds are not signed, so you may not be aware of them as you walk. Look for gently rounded "earthen mounds" along the right side of the trail.

The path takes you near the river and across a small bridge almost immediately. Twenty-three stone steps lead down to the wooden plank bridge and across a small ravine. Just past the bridge is a junction with another trail—continue straight. Notice some crushed rock on the trail as you head uphill now, but not much. The path veers away from the river, but you'll still catch glimpses of it along the way.

After you cross another wooden plank bridge and start a descent, you'll be close to the river again. Ignore the intersecting trails along the way to Ely Ford; stay on the path near the river. There are some tall trees here, including white oak.

When you reach the clearing at Ely Ford, the river commands your attention. Here, the Des Moines River is the widest you've seen it. A large upright stone with a plaque marks this historic spot as the Ely Ford Mormon Crossing. A signboard fills you in on some of the history connected with this site and says: "From the late 1840s to the 1860s an exodus of more than 70,000 Mormons passed by here." A map of the entire Mormon route is shown at the bottom of the signboard. Take a break and relax beneath the large sycamore trees. Imagine Mormons gathered here in the mid-1800s. What were their thoughts as they gazed across the Des Moines River?

When you're ready to hike again, look to the right as you face the river. Across the clearing is a bridge over an inlet—cross it. Now a gentle incline begins. Wild turkeys may dash across your path several times on the walk. Then, after you cross a gully on a natural stone shelf or table rock, the climb becomes steeper. At the top of this cliff, the path continues to ramble up and down. You've moved away from the water, although you can easily hear motorboats on the river.

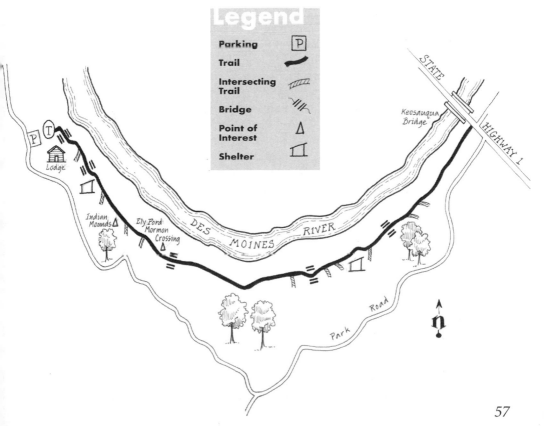

At about 1.35 miles, the path follows a switchback—and now you're back near the river, with a steep drop-off to your left. At the next junction, a sign points out that the Keosauqua Bridge is straight ahead, which is where you are going. As you walk, the natural rock embedded in the path helps with footing on this steep downhill. You'll see shagbark and oak, a typical oak-hickory forest.

Continue to follow the path nearest the river after you cross yet another bridge (over an inlet). Notice the limestone bluffs to the left, along the river. (You also get a nice view of the Keosauqua Bridge, which is the turnaround point of your walk.)

At 1.65 miles, the trail splits off to the right; continue to go straight. After this junction, you'll descend and cross a shallow ravine and then go uphill again. At the next intersection, bear left. About two miles into the walk, notice that the drop-off to the left is quite steep— the river is more than 40 feet below.

Now you're at a clearing that leads up a hill to a shelter area to the right. Do not turn right; continue straight and begin a steep downhill. At the next intersection, take the switchback that veers left, across the wooden plank bridge over an inlet. As the trail continues to descend, you'll begin to see cottonwood.

Soon you're at a timber stand improvement on the right. A sign lets you know that this is native black walnut that took a beating during the flooding of 1993. After the flood, the damaged trees were thinned, which has helped the stand recuperate.

At the next fork in the grassy trail, the sign tells you that the Keosauqua Bridge is about 0.5 mile straight ahead. Continue on. This is another steep uphill climb, with a switchback among rock outcroppings. At the top of the cliff, notice that the path has a lot of natural rock embedded in it. The last 0.5 mile to the bridge is the most rugged—on a foot-wide path.

As you draw nearer to the Keosauqua Bridge, you'll begin a long, steep downhill, probably the steepest of the entire walk. Then a short ascent takes you to the Keosauqua Bridge (the park entrance is here too). After a water break, retrace your steps to the lodge and your car. Watch for deer and wild turkey along the way.

Nature Trails
Lewis and Clark State Park

Distance: 2.45 miles

Time: 1.2 hours

Path: Dirt, grass. This is an easy, level walk through woods and open areas. The park is part of the Lewis and Clark National Historic Trail.

Directions: From Interstate 29 west of Onawa, take State Highway 175 (Exit 112) to Park Loop (the road that winds through the park). Stop and pick up a brochure/map at the park office, then continue on to the parking area near the keelboat sign.

Contact: Lewis and Clark State Park, 21914 Park Loop, Onawa, IA 51040; (712) 423-2829. www.iowadnr.com/parks

Highlights: Imagine walking in the footsteps of early explorers. This park lies on the site where the Lewis and Clark expedition arrived in 1804. Throughout the park, huge cottonwoods soar to the sky. Before or after your hike, hop onto Discovery, the reproduction of Lewis and Clark's own keelboat, for a ride across Blue Lake (part of the Missouri River in the expedition's day). Visit in June during the park's annual Lewis and Clark Festival and relive this era in history with reenactments and more.

Park in the area by the keelboat, then walk across the road to the small kiosk with the Early Explorer Nature Trail sign. Here, pick up a booklet for the interpretive nature trail. (Your walk will cover part of the nature trail, but not all of it.) Facing the kiosk, take the mowed-grass path to your right. Be sure to use plenty of bug spray before you begin.

The mowed-grass path is easy to walk. Interpretive signs dot the trail, pointing out such things as silver maple, snowberries, honey locust, and more. Listen and watch for woodpeckers throughout the walk. You'll come to a junction almost immediately: continue straight. Notice the cottonwood trees too. Soon the wide trail changes to dirt. But the sandy soil is just as comfy to walk on as the grass you left behind.

At about 0.35 mile, bear right at a fork in the trail. Look for hawk feathers on the ground here. At the next junction, turn right again (the nature trail turns left). A trail sign and bench mark this intersection. Now the path leads into a clearing where yellow and purple

59

blooms sway in the breeze and grasses bend low. This path takes you directly to the park road: cross it and pick up the trail on the other side. (A sign here points out that this is a wildlife refuge.)

As you walk the trails, imagine Lewis and Clark roaming the same areas. Trees are farther back from the trail here, but you'll continue to see huge cottonwood—and some red cedar and sumac. At about 0.5 mile turn left (to the right is a camping area). Blue Lake, an oxbow, is to the right (north). In Lewis and Clark's time, this body of water was still part of the Missouri River—and their journey. Look around; beavers have been busy in this area.

Soon you're walking beneath a canopy of cottonwood trees. These impressive giants soar to the sky. Thick patches of horsetail line both sides of the path. Wild grape grows in abundance along many sections of the trail. The grassy path is about 10 feet wide for now, and the trees provide some shade. At about 1 mile into your walk, the path changes back to dirt and narrows at an intersection with a road and a roundabout. Look across the road; you'll see the trailhead (hiker symbol) sign on the other side.

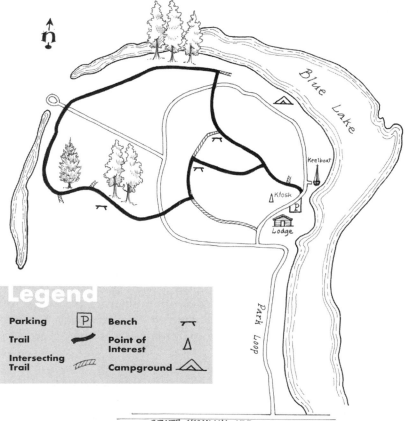

Legend

Parking	P	Bench	⊤
Trail		Point of Interest	Δ
Intersecting Trail		Campground	◺

STATE HIGHWAY 175

The entrance to Lewis and Clark State Park is as scenic as its trails.

Now you're back in a canopy of trees. Watch the roots in the trail here. The awesome cottonwood trees are one of the highlights of this walk. As you come into a clearing, at about 1.35 miles, the path curves sharply to the left (but it's not a junction).

This open area is filled with wild grape, grasses, blooming thistle, and probably plenty of mosquitoes. Sweet-smelling clover grows on the grassy path. The trail winds through this pleasant grassland. Notice red cedar and horsetail, too, but the canopy of trees is gone.

At 1.5 miles, at a junction, continue straight. The path widens to about 14 feet; all around you is wide-open space. Nice! A single row of red cedar lines up, perpendicular to your path. You might see fawns nibbling on vegetation near the trail; they'll look up briefly, then concentrate on their meal again.

Continue straight at the next junction as you head back into cottonwood trees. The trail rambles along for another 0.25 mile, until you reach a park road. Cross it and pick up the trail on the other side (a sign marks the trailhead). You'll need to duck beneath the assertive wild grape—it's taken over this section of the trail.

In another 0.25 mile, bear left at the junction. Soon you'll spot an interpretive sign, pointing out the various vines, including the wild grape you wrestled with earlier. (You're back on part of the nature trail for a short stint.) Signs also point out white ash and red cedar. Take a look at the huge cottonwood tree—the diameter of its trunk must be at least five feet. When you reach the next junction, turn right. The level, seven-foot-wide path wanders through a wooded area, where you'll see honey locust and other trees. Turn right at the next junction too. From this point, you are retracing your steps to the beginning of your walk near the kiosk. Notice again the sandy soil. Be sure to check out the keelboat (and go for a ride) before you leave the park.

North Unit Hike
Effigy Mounds National Monument

Distance: 7.09 miles

Time: 3.5 hours

Path: Boardwalk, crushed rock, wood mulch. Switchbacks and some steep inclines lead to scenic overlooks.

Directions: Travel north from Marquette on State Highway 76, which runs along the Mississippi River. Cross the Yellow River and turn right into the parking area for the Effigy Mounds Visitor Center. (The visitor center is about three miles from Marquette.)

Contact: Effigy Mounds National Monument, 151 State Highway 76, Harpers Ferry, IA 52146-7519; (563) 873-3491. www.nps.gov/efmo

Highlights: Soak up the history of the prehistoric Woodland Culture along the trails as you hike past ancient mounds in the North Unit, including Great Bear Mound, the largest effigy (animal-shaped) mound that exists from this time period. (Effigy mounds were built between 750 to 1,400 years ago.) More than 200 mounds are preserved in the park. This concentration of effigy mounds—shaped like eagles, bears, bison, and other animals important to the Native American culture—is unique to the Mississippi River Valley. Pick up a map at the visitor center—it's detailed and accurate. View the short video about Effigy Mounds, the Woodland culture, and the history of the area. Interpretive signs point to the variety of plants and trees along portions of the trail, including along Fire Point Trail. Signboards also fill in some of the history of the area.

B egin your walk just north of the visitor center on the board-walk, near the white pine and a signboard that explains the "Mystery of the Mounds." This is where you will see the first mounds of the walk as well. (Cone-shaped or conical mounds, used for burial, are the oldest mounds. Linear and compound mounds appeared later and, like effigy mounds, seem to have had ceremonial functions.)

The path turns to crushed rock just past the boardwalk. Interpretive signs dot the trail, identifying plants, flowers, and trees. Depending on the season, you'll see wild geranium, jewelweed, wood nettle, wild mustard, rattlesnake root, and more. Switchbacks take some of the bite out of the steep ascent.

At the first junction, in about 0.25 mile, veer left, continuing on the path to Hanging Rock. Here, wood mulch makes the trail (about five feet wide) comfy to walk on. In the fall, the ground is blanketed with golden bigtooth aspen leaves. You'll also see red oak and maple. A sign points out a bitternut hickory tree nearby.

The next mounds are close by, at about 0.35 mile into the walk. Now the wood mulch on the path gives way to dirt and a bit of crushed rock. A signboard talks about the "river of time," the Mississippi River Valley, and the mounds. Just ahead is a bench that looks over to the river (east) and another mound. (You've ascended more

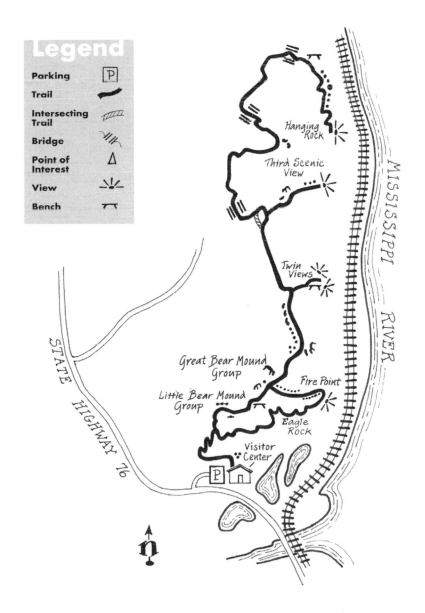

than 250 vertical feet from the beginning of this walk.) The wood mulch begins again.

At about 0.5 mile into your walk is Little Bear Mound. If you've read the information on your park map, you'll know that bears were the most common animal figure associated with effigy mounds in the Midwest. Nearby, the sign at this junction reminds you that Hanging Rock is still up the path—almost 2 miles north—and to allow several hours to get there and back. Continue on. (A right turn would keep you on the Fire Point Trail.) The sign cautions about the steep inclines ahead, and also mentions the reward—scenic vistas. (Take the short paths to the scenic overlooks whenever they're offered —they're worth it.)

Next is Great Bear Mound on the left (west). The massive bear is impressive; it's the largest effigy mound that remains in Iowa, according to the park literature. It's interesting to note that you can see the bear's right side (most of the bears show off their left sides). To the east, walk a short loop to find another bear and a linear mound.

Back on the main trail, continue on past a series of mounds. At the next junction, take a side trip to Twin Views. The signboard offers a glimpse into history, with information about the "Mississippi gorge," which was carved by an ice-age stream. Take in this wonderful view of the Mississippi and the Hanging Rock (north view). Notice the dome-shaped mound here (near the south view). Relax on the bench.

When you've had your fill of vistas, continue on the northerly path to Hanging Rock. The trail is mostly dirt and grass at this point, with a few remnants of crushed rock. Note the stand of aspen. As you walk, also notice the sections of tallgrass prairie to the west. The path has started to pop up a few tree roots, so watch your step. In the fall, rusty red oak and sumac add color to the landscape.

At about 1.65 miles, several connecting junctions pop up (not seen on the park map). Take the "Third Scenic View" path to the right (watch for the mounds), then backtrack to the main trail, still on your way to Hanging Rock. Now you'll start a descent, down and around a ravine.

By the time you hit 2.50 miles, you've probably figured out that this is a steep, challenging section of trail with plenty of ups and downs. Soon you're at a plank bridge, where the path starts to ascend. You won't see any mounds for a while. Notice the shagbark hickory.

At 2.75 miles, you'll see two mounds to the right (east), just a few steps off the main path. Now you'll descend, with a series of switchbacks. Stop for a moment at the small bridge and enjoy the quiet. You're in a low spot; trees surround you, and noises from the outside world are muffled. (You've descended about 117 vertical feet from the first bench and overlook on this walk.) Not as many visitors continue on to Hanging Rock, so chances are you will only meet up with a few hikers. At this bridge, there is more of the same up-and-down climbing.

Cross another bridge at about 3.5 miles. This plank bridge is about 20 feet long. As you ascend, notice the rustic wooden fence with a log railing. As you climb, you're already getting some nice overlooks of the Mississippi. The path's wood mulch is quite thick here.

Just before Hanging Rock, you'll reach another series of mounds (and a bench). The trail is crushed rock again, just a few feet wide, sort of a switchback, followed by a steep descent from the rock outcropping you just climbed. You'll drop about 52 vertical feet in the span of about a hundred yards.

At about 3.8 miles, you're at Hanging Rock. Wow. You can see Twin Views from here. Look down the Mississippi River, at the Prairie du Chien Bridge, islands in the middle of the river, and several boats. Notice the red cedar near the top. Enjoy the spectacular vistas. In autumn the fall colors and cool breezes are a bonus when walking these trails and gazing out at the overlooks.

When you're ready, retrace your steps back to the Fire Point Trail junction that you did not take on the way up (near Little Bear Mound, about 0.5 mile from the beginning of your walk). At this junction, go left. As you walk uphill, notice the series of conical mounds along the trail. Stop at the interpretive signboard, which explains how the mounds were created, how bodies were laid out for burial, and the accompanying ceremonies.

The trail follows along the edge of the bluff, staying high. Look for barges on the river. As you curve around a bend, catch the sun streaming through the golden aspen in late afternoon in autumn. Admire the thick stand of aspen, with tall, straight trees glowing with color. Beautiful! In fact, it's just one big scenic overlook along here.

Just slightly more than 6.5 miles into the walk, you'll have reached the junction with the main trail. The steep switchbacks back to the visitor center are just as ornery on the way down: your toes are jammed into the front of your shoes as you descend. Your walk ends at the visitor center. A soda machine out front may call to you now.

Ready for More?
Stay another day in the area and hike the South Unit to the Marching Bear Group.

South Unit Hike
Effigy Mounds National Monument

Distance: 5.45 miles

Time: 3 hours

Path: Gravel, wood chips, grass. The wide trails are well marked and easy to follow.

Directions: From Marquette, travel north on State Highway 76 for about three miles. (This also is part of the Great River Road along the Mississippi River.) You'll see the visitor center on your right, shortly after crossing the Yellow River.

Contact: Effigy Mounds National Monument, 151 Highway 76, Harpers Ferry, IA 52146-7519; (563) 873-3491. www.nps.gov/efmo

Highlights: The Marching Bear Group is considered a sacred place. A hike to this area and other mounds in the South Unit is an experience you won't forget.

S top at the visitor center for a map and information about the trails in the South Unit (and to pay the modest user fee). Displays, books, and even hiking sticks are available at the center. Then backtrack in your car a short distance to pick up the South Unit trails. Turn left from the parking lot and cross the Yellow River again. Just past the bridge, a sign on the left indicates the Yellow River boat access and South Unit parking, 200 feet ahead.

Park here, beside the Mississippi. Directly across the highway is the trailhead; you can see the gate from the parking area. Begin your walk at the trailhead sign: Marching Bear and Nezekaw Point Trail Access. The first mile of trail is uphill—and rather steep for about 0.5 mile. The rest of the climb is more gradual. The trail, about 10 to 12 feet wide, is in a heavily wooded area; notice the oaks and maples as you walk.

At about 0.5 mile, you'll reach the junction with Nezekaw Point Trail to the right. This path is deeply covered with wood chips. For now, stay on the main trail, heading for the Marching Bear Group. (Explore this side trail another time, or on the way back if you wish.) When you've gone about 1 mile on the trail, you'll come to another junction on the right. This is not a signed trail, but the wood-chip path leads to a mound just a few hundred yards away. After you visit the mound, continue on.

Soon you'll enter an open prairie area: black-eyed Susan, butterfly milkweed, and red cedar greet you. Notice the grass trail to the left (east). This trail leads to the Compound Mound Group; pick it up on your way back. Now the gravel on the trail is deeper.

At 1.5 miles, another wood-chip trail takes off to the left. Go straight; don't turn. Now you're back in woods again. In another 0.25 mile, you might glimpse part of a linear mound through the trees on your left as you approach the Marching Bear Group. When you've

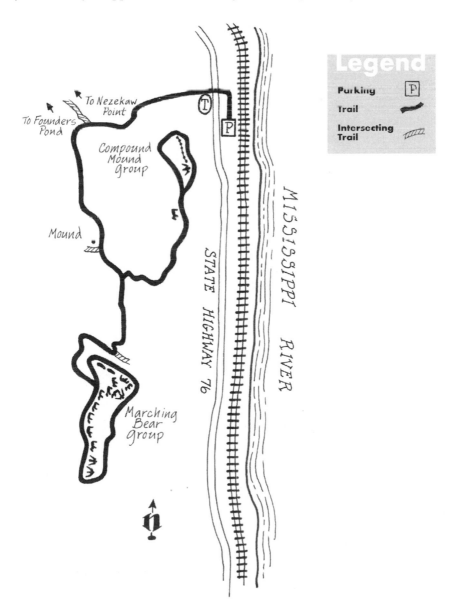

walked almost two miles, you'll reach the clearing that leads to the Marching Bears. Here, you'll find two linear mounds, 10 bear mounds, and three bird mounds. This is a sacred place. Treat it with reverence, in honor of the ancient people who created these mounds.

The birds face the river, as if they could fly toward it; the bears have their feet toward the river. Walk along the group, on both sides, to appreciate the size and scope of the mounds. Past the group to the south is a fence and boundary line; a farmer's field lies beyond. Spend some time up here before you return to the path. Sit beneath one of the large oaks that stand guard, as if protecting this special place from unseen forces. Listen to the wind as it blows along the ridge and imagine the spirits telling the story of a time past, of their bond to nature.

When you're ready to return to the path, retrace your steps to the Compound Mound Group trail junction. You've walked about 2.5 miles now as you start back down the trail. In slightly more than 0.5 mile, you'll reach a junction, a 14-foot-wide grassy trail on your right, with a stand of aspen just beyond. The grassy trail gives way to deep wood chips as you walk a slight descent. Now the path is about 10 feet wide.

A bear mound comes into sight first. Then you'll see a bird, the largest bird effigy at this national monument. The compound mound just beyond is the largest compound mound as well. You can see the Mississippi River and hear the sound of boats. Here, too, it seems as if the bird is ready to take flight over the water.

Then retrace your steps to the intersection and bear right. Now you're on the main gravel trail; follow this back to the trailhead and then to the parking area and your car.

The spiritual nuances of this place will remain with you long after this hike is over.

Ready for More?

Hike another South Unit trail to the Nezekaw Point Overlook (about 2 miles round trip from the trailhead/gate).

Loops by Lakes

Red Haw State Park

Ancient Pine and Lake Walk
Pine Lake State Park

Distance:	4.01 miles
Time:	2.75 hours
Path:	Cement, crushed rock, dirt.
Directions:	From State Highway 175 just east of Eldora, turn north onto County Road S56. From the east, a sign announces Pine Lake State Park about 1 mile before you reach the turnoff. The entrance is a stone portal with a park sign. As you enter the park, drive past the river access, picnic area, and cabins until you reach a sign that tells you beach parking is to the left. Park here. Walk toward another beach sign and an underpass that leads you directly to the beach area.
Contact:	Pine Lake State Park, 22620 County Road S56, Eldora, IA 50627-8010; (641) 858-5832. www.iowadnr.com/parks
Highlights:	Towering white pines, two lakes, and easy-to-walk trails through woods and near the shore make this park a pleasant place to spend a few hours. Take your time—enjoy!

Begin your walk at the stone-covered underpass near the parking area. After the underpass, the path leads to the open shelter near the beach. Ignore the dirt service road on your left that leads to a camping area. At the sidewalk south of the shelter, turn left. Several large cottonwood trees welcome you to the trail. In autumn, colorful maples highlight this picturesque lakeside path. Look across the water at the huge white pines (one pine is more than 200 years old) on the south shore of Lower Pine Lake.

Several sets of benches placed next to the lake are perfect for watching waterfowl. At different times of the year you may see a wood duck, a teal, a mallard, or a Canada goose skimming along the water. Here, the path looks like it was sliced out of a hill (on the left). Notice the exposed natural stone and the flowers. In the fall, there is colorful sumac too. Trees on the hillside tilt toward the lake—an interesting effect.

In about 0.5 mile, cross a wooden plank bridge in a marshy area with cattails on both sides of the path. After the bridge, the path veers away from the lake, and you'll start a series of gentle ups and downs. Watch for red-headed woodpeckers—they're abundant in this park, and especially visible in the fall. Turkey vultures are common too.

About a mile into your walk, you'll reach a spillway. Look down and see if you can spot a silvery flash of fish in the water. At the spill-

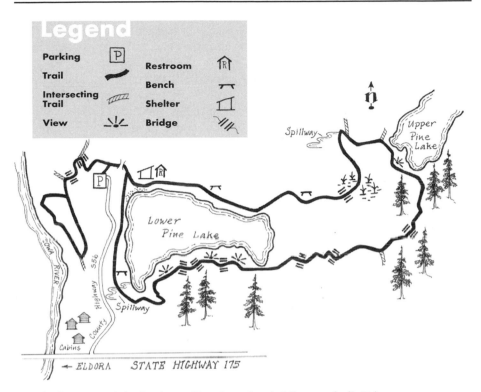

Legend

Parking	P	Restroom	ℝ
Trail		Bench	ᵔ
Intersecting Trail		Shelter	
View		Bridge	

way, look to your right for the trailhead marker (a hiker symbol). Take this crushed-rock/dirt trail. (If you had continued on the cement path, it would lead to a camping area and boat rental—a nice place for a picnic or a break, with a spigot for refilling water bottles.)

The trail has now become six feet wide, and the first section heads uphill. Watch out for large rocks and tree roots along the way. Soon you're above the spillway, looking down on Upper Pine Lake. Nice view! (You've climbed about 150 vertical feet since the beginning of your walk.) Breathe in the fresh scent of pines that are scattered on both sides of the trail. At the Y-intersection, turn right. Woodpeckers continue to make their presence known—here, you might see downy and red-headed woodpeckers. There are lots of snags, too, among the shagbark hickory and oak. Leave the lake and pines behind and start a descent. The trail narrows as you move into bottomland forest, where you'll see silver maple too.

At about 1.25 miles, the trail curves to the right to avoid a soggy area. Next, you'll come to a creek and a water control structure, informally known as the "turtle dam," that helps with erosion. Notice that paper birches have been cut down on the hillside. Soon, you'll cross a wooden plank bridge over a wash.

Now begin a winding ascent. White pine makes an appearance again—along with plenty of their long, curved cones. When you've gone about 1.5 miles, you'll see a path to the left that leads to a group camp. Don't take it. But stop and enjoy the scenic view, looking down at the lake below. Listen for owls. The path follows the curve of the lake, although you are still above it. As you meander up and down on the path for another mile, you'll come to a several sections with railroad-tie steps—more than 200 in all. And you'll cross five bridges. Several of the bridges are unique: a mix of wood, stone buttresses, and arches. Many of the bridges in the park were built by the Civilian Conservation Corps in the 1930s.

At times, a moss-covered stone retaining wall juts out to meet the path. Be sure to stop at one of the scenic lookouts along this stretch. Some lookout platforms are cushioned with a deep layer of pine needles and cones. At one lookout, you'll need to crane your neck around a giant pine to see the lake. The stately pines are old; one pine is believed to be more than 200 years old. Boulders line the outside edge of the path at times, which alerts you to the steep drop to the water below. Notice the paper birch here too.

Once you're past a double-decker observation platform at about 2.25 miles, you'll cross an inlet on a boardwalk. This section of the trail ends at a parking area and a road at about 2.5 miles. Look at the massive cottonwood tree here.

Now turn right and cross the spillway on a concrete path near the shore of the lower lake. Follow the path back to the beach and shelter at the beginning of the walk.

At the shelter, take the path back through the underpass to the parking area and your car. But don't end your walk here! Follow the road west; you'll see a trailhead and hiker sign on the edge of parking area. As you descend onto the narrow, rocky path, note the ravine on the left, and a hill to the right. In the fall, gaze down into the ravine at honey-colored maples topped by an azure sky—beautiful! Leaves flutter down from the trees like confetti.

When you reach a junction at a stone footbridge, bear left and follow the leaf-covered path to another intersection and bridge (turn left). In just a few minutes you'll be at another junction. Do not turn right; continue on. In the fall, it's easy to miss some of these junctions because the paths are leaf-covered.

Now you'll see a grassy ridge to the left and a slope with trees on the right. At the T-intersection, turn right. (If you went straight ahead, you would end up in the Iowa River.) The path widens to about 10 feet across as you walk along the river's edge. Look across the river at a beautiful tree-topped ridge. In autumn, citrus-colored maples are reflected in the water.

At about 3.65 miles, the grassy path turns away from river. Soon you're at the end of a loop. Turn left and simply retrace your steps to the trailhead and parking area.

Lake of Three Fires Hike
Lake of Three Fires State Park

Distance: 5.21 miles

Time: 3.5 hours

Path: Dirt, some gravel/crushed rock. The multiuse trails in the park are often uneven and muddy. It's easy to see where horses' hooves have sunk into the soft ground after a rain. In wet weather, the trail is almost impassable in low areas. This hike isn't a stroll, and you will get dirty. But if you think a challenge is half the fun, then this trail is for you. Wear hiking boots, preferably weatherproof ones.

Directions: From State Highway 2 east of Bedford, turn north on Lake Road. Follow this road (about two miles) to the entrance of the park. As you enter the park, note the signs that direct you to the campground, picnic area, beach, etc. The park office is on your right; pick up a brochure and ask about trail conditions. Then take the curve to the left and park your car on the roundabout in the direction of the beach.

Contact: Lake of Three Fires State Park, 2303 Lake Road, Bedford, IA 50833; (712) 523-2700. www.iowadnr.com/parks

Highlights: A mix of shaded and sunlit trails along a rolling terrain. The multiuse paths can be challenging after heavy rains. But glimpses of wildlife, along with secluded paths that loop around a lake and ramble through woods and a meadow, make it worth the effort.

The trailhead is visible from the roundabout where you've parked. Look across the grassy area toward the east (the sign only has an equestrian symbol, but it is a multiuse trail).

Begin your walk on this six-feet-wide dirt path. Think twice about hiking after heavy rains—you'll sink in mud. A walking stick or poles come in handy and might mean the difference between slipping and sliding down a hill or striding along at a good pace.

The park's brochure contains some history about the park, including the interesting legend behind its name. It is said that three tribes formed an alliance known as Three Fires after a great council meeting in southern Iowa. As long as the three fires kept burning, the alliance between the three tribes was intact. (One of the fires was at a point now covered by the lake.)

You'll see red cedar, oak, and sumac in the first 0.25 mile. As the trail curves, notice the rock and clay tile pieces on the path. At an intersection with a service road to the right, bear left and follow the trail. After you cross a bridge at about 0.5 mile, you'll be at a junction with a detailed signboard. The signboard's "You Are Here" feature pinpoints exactly where you are on the trail and gives mileage! Turn right on the Lakeside Trail for now—a shaded 10-foot-wide path. Notice the honey locust pods, along with deer tracks on the trail.

At the next fork in the path turn right, as you draw closer to the lake. Soon, you'll reach a clearing with the spillway and a bridge just ahead (and finally, a good view of the lake). Another signboard displays the different lake loops and even the shortcuts by the ponds. Turn left here. Continue on to the next junction and bear right (stay on the path closest to the lake). Notice the lily pads floating on the lake. Every so often, grass crops up on the trail.

Next, you'll be at the junction where the Outside Trail hooks up

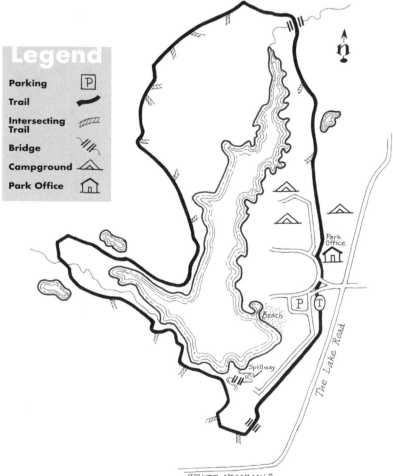

Legend

Parking   P

Trail

Intersecting Trail

Bridge

Campground

Park Office

Park Office

Beach

Spillway

The Lake Road

STATE HIGHWAY 2

with the Lakeside Trail (you're leaving the Lakeside Trail). Turn right. As you turn, another "You Are Here" signboard reminds you of the miles to go. Now walk across the grassy dam (a pond is to your left). Enjoy the unexpected open meadow brimming with black-eyed Susans and other wildflowers to the right.

Then you're back in the woods on a gentle uphill. At almost 2 miles, you'll hit another clearing, and then it's downhill. (Note the boundary line to the left.) Slews of wild raspberries crowd the trail; you'll also see some red cedar. At this point, the path isn't near the lake. At about 2.25 miles, cross another grassy dam. A pond is on your left, and an open field is to the right. Now you're close to the lake—admire the lily pads. Notice shagbark hickory and oak too. Go straight at the next junction; don't turn right. There is quite of bit of natural rock embedded in the very muddy path. Pick your steps carefully.

At about 3 miles, you'll spot another great signboard. Continue on the Outside Trail (straight). The path is wide and grassy now as it wanders in and out of woods for the next 0.25 mile. Go straight at the next junction and enjoy the gentle uphill through a clearing.

The next intersection is a two-prong deal. A loop joins up here, so you will see two grassy paths on the right in close proximity. The signboard is near the second path. Continue straight. (The loop to the right takes you close to the lake, but it also adds mileage.)

Ah, this is a pretty intersection. If you're lucky, you'll note the birds singing, fluffy clouds floating by, black-eyed Susans swaying in the breeze, deer scrambling across the path. It's one of those idyllic moments that even makes the mud seem worthwhile. The next 0.5 mile continues to be the nicest part of the walk. Enjoy the pastoral setting, the rolling hills, and the wildflowers. Soon, you'll reach another junction with two trails off to the right (another loop joins up here). The signboard is at the second path—continue straight.

At about 4 miles, bear left at the intersection (with a signboard). This descent will be muddy. The road on your left is visible through the trees. You may see more deer bounding along. At about 4.25 miles, cross a wooden plank bridge over a creek. A great blue heron rises from the water as you reach the other side.

Continue straight at the next junction too. This is a steep uphill but not an intimidating one. Notice the large white oak and some shagbark hickory. Soon, pass by another pond to the left. At another junction (at 4.75 miles), continue straight.

Just past this, the trail comes out to the road; note the campground on your right. Walk on the road and pass by the equestrian campground on the left—and more campground to the right of this road. Walk in the grass beside the road where there's plenty of room. At about 5 miles into the walk, you'll meet another road: turn left toward the park office, then back to the roundabout and your car.

Redbud Walk
Red Haw State Park

Distance: 5.12 miles

Time: 2.4 hours

Path: Wide, mowed-grass path, about 10 feet wide. This easy, level trail loops partway around a 72-acre lake. The grass disappears occasionally, but most of the path is a lush, green carpet, especially in the spring when you'll also be walking beneath a canopy of flowering redbud trees.

Directions: Travel east from Chariton on U.S. Highway 34. Note the Red Haw sign shortly after leaving the city limits. In about 1 mile, turn right (south) into the signed park entrance. Huge white pines line the right (west) side of the road. Follow the road to the other end of the park until you can't drive any further. Park off the loop near the restroom, just above the lake.

Contact: Red Haw State Park, 24550 U.S. Highway 34, Chariton, IA 50049; (641) 774-5632. www.iowadnr.com/parks

Highlights: Oh, when the redbud trees are in bloom! It's a spectacular sight: cotton-candy pink treetops fluffed against a sapphire sky. Patches of mayapples, a glimpse of a fox and other wildlife—and even an unexpected spring shower—also make this hike worthwhile. Most likely, you'll have the wildlife to yourself on this quiet walk.

Park your car at the end of the road (off the small loop by the restroom), then walk down the hill to the lake. Near the water's edge, look to the right (south) for a wide, grassy path. Although the trailhead isn't marked, it's not difficult to find.

Now stroll beneath a canopy of redbud trees. What a wonderful way to start a hike! The path is salted with redbud blossoms; sweet williams and wild raspberries add to the mix. Not only can you admire the redbud trees above and around you, look across the lake and see the beauties on the opposite shore as well.

At about 0.35 mile, the path curves left—stay with it. (To the right, a service road heads up the hill, but don't take it.) Here, you'll walk across a small grassy dam on the south end of the lake's finger. After the curve, an intersecting path on the right leads up a hill. Don't take it; continue on the same trail.

Blue jays are as abundant as the wild raspberries. Take a break on the bench that follows and gaze out over the lake. Canada geese honk nearby. At times, the path loses its grass covering, but it's still a comfortable trail. Here and there, a few roots sidle onto the path, so watch your step.

As the redbud trees fade out for a bit, the trail widens to almost 20 feet. You'll have a slight ascent here too. At about 0.75 mile, the path joins up with another trail to the right. Follow the original trail—go straight. Mayapples continue to pop up as the trail winds along the lakeshore.

About a mile into the walk, cross a grassy dam on yet another finger of the lake. Notice the boggy area to the right; the lake is on the left. At the next junction turn left to keep on the path nearest the lake.

Now the trail is quite grassy again and back to about 10 feet wide. Ah, your feet are really pampered on this walk. A large cottonwood on the left commands your attention. At 1.25 miles, at another junction, go straight, still next to the lake. You'll see more wild raspberries along here. If you visit in early May to see the redbud trees bloom, you'll need to return later in the season for the berries.

U.S. HIGHWAY 34

Legend

Parking	P
Trail	➤
Intersecting Trail	▦
Bench	⌐
View	☀
Restroom	🛉

**What's better than a springtime stroll beneath a canopy
of redbud trees at Red Haw State Park?**

Walk beneath another canopy of redbud trees at about 1.35 miles.
Red columbine grows along here too. After a brief shower, the large
patches of mayapples will glisten as redbud blossoms rain down.

At about 1.5 miles, follow the slight downhill as the trail curves
away from the lake. At the next junction, turn left (a boundary line is
straight ahead). Turn left again almost immediately. Deer paths are
abundant and, depending on the time of day, so are the deer. You
might spot a fox on a trail, its bushy tail disappearing around the next
curve. In spring, you'll continue to see red columbine and countless
mayapples—some really tall ones! The pale sweet william blossoms are
easy to find along here too. At about 1.75 miles, stop and look across
the water; it's a great view of all the redbud trees framing the lake.

At about 2 miles, a bench provides an excuse to check out another
lake vista. The next junction pops up soon after this; turn left. (If you
go straight, the trail dead-ends.) Now cross the grassy dam, heading
to the beach. It's very scenic here too: look across the lake on the left.
Notice that the dam runs parallel to U.S. Highway 34.

After you step off the dam, pick up the path near the lake (look
thorough an opening in the trees to find it). If you happen to walk
past it, simply head for the beach. Although the beach house is closed,
the beach area is still accessible. If you have lunch or a snack in your
daypack, this is the spot to dine. Note the boat rental shack here too.

When you're ready, retrace your steps across the dam, along the
lake, and to your car. The redbud trees are just as impressive on the
way back.

Springbrook Stroll
Springbrook State Park

Distance: 3.24 miles

Time: 1.75 hours

Path: Gravel and dirt paths wind along the lake and into woods. Look for birds—there are many!

Directions: From Panora, take State Highway 4 north to County Road F25, and turn west there. A sign tells you the park is about 5 miles away. Continue on past the conservation office. As you enter the park area, you'll see a wooden sign; past this is a stone pillar and another sign. Follow the directional signs to the beach and parking area.

Contact: Springbrook State Park, 2437 160th Road, Guthrie Center, IA 50115; (641) 747-3591. www.iowadnr.com/parks

Highlights: A scenic park with many trails. Bring a backpack with a lunch and enjoy it in one of the picturesque picnic areas. Watch for scarlet tanagers and other colorful birds. The wooded path may be sprinkled with snails in the spring, an interesting sight. A red fox may even cross your path.

Begin your walk near the shelter house on the beach, just a few steps down from the parking area. As you face the lake, look toward the right for the trail.

The gravel trail, about six feet wide, follows along the edge of the lake. In a couple hundred feet you will be at a fishing dock. Notice the shagbark hickory and oak in the woods to the right. You'll see sweet william and red columbine in the spring. Benches are placed near the water, so you can stop and gaze out over the serene lake.

When you've gone about 0.2 mile, you'll be looking down on the lake; you've gained some altitude. The lake is to your left, and on the right is a sloping, wooded hill. The gravel path can be quite wet here, but a boardwalk gets you past the wet area in good shape. Now you're at the head of the lake; a small brook runs through a marshy area to the north/northeast. Notice more patches of red columbine joined by Virginia waterleaf. You'll also see plenty of good-sized white oak trees. There are lots of snags in the wooded area to the right.

The bench here is an interesting, split-log seat. Now you've gone about 0.35 mile. All that is left of the water view is the small stream or creek; there is no lake view now. Erosion has crept up on the path along here. Tree roots hang out from a steep bank on the right. Some

Legend

Parking	P	Restroom	⛨
Trail	➴	Bench	⊤
Intersecting Trail	▨	Shelter	⌂
View	☀	Bridge	⌇
Point of Interest	△	Picnic Area	⛺

of the trees look as if they could topple over.

Now the path is thick with red, sandy dirt. Crumbling rock formations appear to have contributed to this carpet of sand. Near the creek to the left, you'll see cottonwood and some red oak. At 0.5 mile, turn right and head up a hill in an easterly direction. Here you may see snails along the trail; the snails are good-sized, with a variegated brown-and-tan shell. This section of the trail is mostly dirt. You've traveled about 0.1 mile and climbed about 100 vertical feet. Look down into ravines on both sides now. At about 0.75 mile, you'll reach a road that loops around a camping/picnic area. This is a beautiful spot with a large expanse of mowed grass. Red-headed woodpeckers flit from tree to tree. What a great spot for a picnic.

Follow the loop left until you reach the trailhead sign (on the left with a hiker symbol). The trail is almost as wide as an access road. Notice lots of shagbark hickory. At about 1 mile, turn left at a fork in the path. To the left is a barbed-wire fence—a boundary. Look down at the pastoral view below. Nice!

Lots of deer tracks crisscross the path. Look around; you should see several on your walk. A cardinal calls in a nearby tree. Now a trail takes off to the right. Do not turn; continue straight. The secluded trail is serene; listen to birds instead of traffic. You'll likely have the trails to yourself. Now the path curves and starts to loop back. Large, gnarled oaks give the woods some added character. Listen to the breeze waft in and out of the trees, along with the birds' voices. A scarlet tanager's brilliant color flashes nearby.

At about 1.5 miles, you'll reach a junction with another trail to the right. (This is the other end of the trail that cuts through the middle of this loop.) Go straight. The wide path (no rocks or roots!) meanders up and down; you might see the snails on the trail again. Deer run across your path.

At almost 2 miles, you're back at the end of the loop. Return to the park road, turn right, and retrace your steps to the lakeside path (turn right onto the trail). Back at the lake, turn right again (to loop around the lake). Soon the trail crosses over a small stream. To the right is grassland. As the path curves around the lake, you'll see oak on the hillside to the right. Notice the sweet william and red columbine. At about 2.5 miles, you'll cross a ravine. Now you once again have a view of the lake on the left, where the stream joins the lake.

Shagbark hickory and white oak are thick on the hillside to the right. Stop at the bench and empty the rocks from your shoes. Here, take a spur trail to a little finger of land that juts out into the lake, complete with a bench. Another scenic spot (with a bench) is just ahead. Baltimore orioles are often around this area. Notice the cottonwoods too.

The wooded lake path comes to an end on the southwest corner of the lake. To finish your loop, walk in the grass on the left side of the road, past a dock and a boat ramp. You are now directly above another park road (below is the campground store, playground, etc.). Now walk across the spillway bridge to the shelter house and beach area. You've completed your lake loop.

Swan Lake Loop
Swan Lake State Park

Distance: 3.87 miles

Time: 1.75 hours

Path: An asphalt trail loops around Swan Lake. Although this trail is part of the Sauk Rail Trail system, it is not an actual rail-to-trail path

Directions: From U.S. Highway 71 south of Carroll, turn east onto 220th Street (County Road E37). In about 2 miles, you'll enter Swan Lake State Park on Swan Lake Drive. Look for a parking lot to the left (at the intersection of Swan Lake Drive and Swan Lake Road). Near the parking area is a yellow post for your trail fee ($1 per day per hiker/rider). After you park, you'll need to cross Swan Lake Road to reach the trailhead. The trail is marked Sauk Rail Trail.

Contact: Carroll County Conservation Board, 22676 Swan Lake Drive, Carroll, IA 51401; (712) 792-4614.
Sac County Conservation Board, 2970 280th Street, Sac City, IA 50583; (712) 662-4530. www.saccounty.org

Highlights: A fun loop around Swan Lake. The asphalt path is an easy stroll in spring, summer, and fall—and even in winter.

Before you walk, be sure to put your $1 user fee in the yellow post near the parking area. Then cross Swan Lake Road to access the trail. As you walk the wide trail, notice the marshy area on the left. At about 0.35 mile you'll cross a small bridge.

In the spring and summer, goldfinches flit across the trail and near large silver maples. Soon, farms, pastures, and fields are spread out before you. At the first junction with a road (at 0.5 mile), cross the road and continue on. Notice the bridle path to the right.

This is a low area; red cedar lines the path on the left. As you cross several gravel roads, continue to pick up the trail on the other side. At about 1.35 miles, you'll reach an intersection with a hard-surface park road. Now you'll get glimpses of the lake as you stroll on the gently rolling path. After the next gravel road, notice the large grassy park area (to the right) with a volleyball net and planted pines.

At about 1.65 miles, you'll be at the entrance to the East Shelter House. Enjoy the scenic view of the lake and beach area. A nearby picnic area is perfect for a break. Stroll along the lakeshore: trees shade the path and benches are placed every hundred feet or so. Watch for Canada geese on the lake. Notice wildlife pen #3 across the road.

(Several more wildlife pens are along here too.) The "zoo" has elk, deer, and sheep most of the time. There is also a butterfly garden across the road at about 2 miles.

Now cross a bridge over a stream that drains into the lake. Look ahead, there's a small hill to climb. After you've gone uphill for a bit, you will come to another junction with a park road; notice the yellow gates.

Continue on the trail; the glittering lake is still to the right. This is a popular area near the water, and there's always activity. Watch people fish, stroll, bike, picnic, or relax near the beach.

The trail continues uphill and pulls away from the lake. Several grassy ski trails shoot off from your asphalt path; ignore them. As the trail curves, enjoy the expanse of farmers' fields that pops into view. Now you'll come to a marshy area where you will see horsetail. Then enter a canopy of trees and go downhill. Pass through another set of yellow gates at the intersection with the park road. To the left is the park's concession stand, which is open seasonally. Stop if you wish. You've gone about 3 miles now. Notice the large white oak here. Look to the right and see paddleboats on the lake (you can rent one when you're through with this walk (check with the park for seasonal availability).

The shaded path winds through the park past a play area, picnic area, and benches. Everyone you meet has a smile, and you probably do too. The path joins the park road near a camping area with large oak trees. Follow the campground road as it veers right through the camping area for about 0.35 mile. Then pick up the actual trail for a short distance until you see the parking lot and your car.

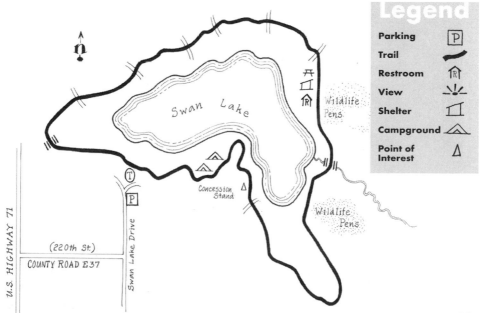

Water and Woodland Walk
Geode State Park

Distance: 7.53 miles

Time: 4 hours

Path: Dirt, some crushed rock/gravel, grass, and park road. The paths are rugged at times, with switchbacks, hills, and ravines.

Directions: From Burlington, take U.S. Highway 34 west to County Road 79 (old State Highway 79). Continue west on County Road 79 for about 8 miles directly into the park.

Contact: Geode State Park, 3249 Racine Avenue, Danville, IA 52623; (319) 392-4601. www.iowadnr.com/parks

Highlights: Chances are that you won't find any geodes as you hike the trails around the lake. But the scenic lake views, quiet woods, and meandering trails make this a worthwhile hike. Tuck a lunch in your daypack and enjoy it at one of the picnic areas.

Park in the large parking lot near the beach and head in a northerly direction to the marked trailhead near the lagoon. The gravel path is about five feet wide as you begin walking in a wooded area with oak, hickory, some maple, and ironwood. (This is part of the interpretive trail; a brochure is available at the park office.) After you cross a ravine, a signboard illustrates the park's watershed, and a bench overlooks the lagoon. Here, also notice a patch of mayapple.

Now the path changes to more of a crushed-rock surface and narrows a bit. As you move deeper into the woods, the trail simply becomes a dirt path. Throughout the hike, you will cross ravines and meander up and down switchbacks.

As you descend, the path gets muddy and more uneven. At about 0.5 mile, you'll notice more understory trees. The lagoon is on the left; this is a low, muddy area. In a few minutes you'll reach a clearing. Walk into the clearing past the turnaround loop; turn onto the road and head in an easterly direction.

Next, cross a small stone bridge onto a different road, one that winds through the park. Here, turn left and cross another bridge over a creek. After the second bridge, look left and you will see the trailhead sign. Pick up the path here, and head back into the woods in a westerly direction.

The damp path is about three feet wide now. The soil has quite a bit of clay in it, and the bedrock is not far below the clay. You are under a canopy of trees, with some maple, basswood, and oak. The lake is gone from your sight in this low area, with a ridge to the left and a hill to the right. Now it's an uphill climb; when you reach the top of the ridge, you'll have hiked about 1 mile. The trees are large—about 40 to 50 feet tall. There are also quite a few snags in the woods.

Soon, you'll encounter another switchback as you go up and down ravines. Enjoy the quiet, the sunlight streaming through the trees, birds singing. The path widens, then narrows frequently. The trail is often washed out in the middle, making the path a little tricky to navigate.

At about 1.35 miles, the trail leads into a clearing with a picnic

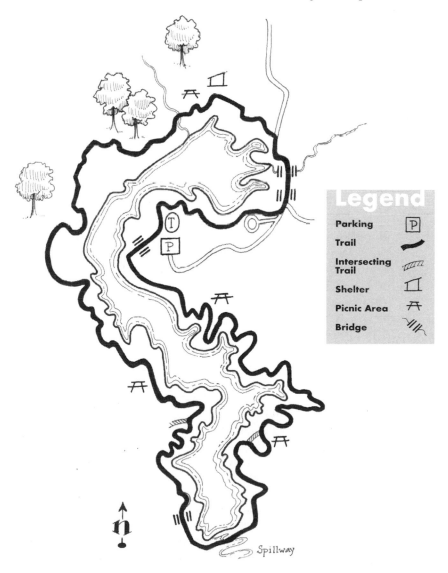

area. Head toward the stone shelter house (Shelter #1 on the park map); just beyond it you'll find the trailhead and path. Huge white oaks tower above as you descend the steep, slick trail with plenty of rock protruding. Many of the second-generation trees near the shelter are part of the original park, according to the park manager, most likely planted in the 1870s.

At about 1.5 miles, cross a narrow, shallow creek. Weatherproof hiking boots will keep your feet dry. This area is littered with rocks of all sizes, perhaps even a geode. Now it's back to an uphill climb. The path is embedded with rocks and often washed out in the middle. As the trail curves west, notice the shagbark hickory. Although this incline isn't particularly steep, it is long—more than 0.25 mile.

When you reach a fence at a boundary line, veer south (the only way to go). The now-grassy trail almost fades away; a sign says the sewage stabilization lagoon is to the right. Sample a few wild raspberries in this more open area. Shortly, you will start a downhill climb; the trail is slick, still washed out in the middle, and then turns back to dirt. At the bottom of the ravine look for ferns and start another climb.

At about 2 miles, a fence line marks the west boundary. There are more rolling hills and ridges through here. Wildflowers and clover grow thick, taking advantage of a few scattered openings in the woods. Notice the cottonwood too. Continue uphill; the path gets drier as you ascend. At about 2.5 miles, you'll come upon a row of volunteer red cedar and more wildflowers. Then it's back to a canopy of trees—and a downhill. Savor the solitude—you might only meet one person on all the trails.

Soon, the trail bottoms out at about 600 feet elevation (the lake is back in view!). Watch your footing in this low spot. Then you'll climb about 52 vertical feet in a short distance. Large rocks in the path help with footing on the way up. Look for deer running near the path. Walk up and down another ravine at about 3 miles into the walk.

Next, you'll arrive at a picnic area by the lake. Relax on this breezy hillside that slopes down to the lake. It's a great spot for lunch, a snack, or a water break. You might not want to leave this idyllic spot near Shelter #4.

To pick up the trail again, head for the lake and an opening in the trees—where there is a trailhead sign. The dirt path follows along the side of the lake for a short distance, and then heads back into the woods. A sign that says Lake Trail (with an arrow) leads the way. The path is two feet wide now; you'll see maple, oak, and shagbark hickory. The trail continues to meander up and down some healthy hills.

At the next junction, take the trail that nudges you toward the lake. At about 4 miles, you'll walk on a natural table rock across a ravine— fun! The path keeps on with its up-and-down pattern. Soon, a wooden plank bridge leads to a lakeside picnic area. At 4.35 miles, you'll reach the spillway dam. Walk across the dam on the mowed-grass path beside the road, then pick up the trail on the other side (look to an opening in the brush on the left). Stay on this path near the lake.

Cross another ravine with a table rock, along a switchback. At about 4.75 miles, you're at another picnic area. Take a lower path near the lake here or simply walk across the picnic area and pick up the path near a trailhead sign.

Now you'll descend. Notice the piles of rock strewn everywhere: at the bases of trees, on the hillside, and near the lake too. At about 5.35 miles, you're at another switchback; the dirt trail is about three feet wide as you cross several ravines. At about 5.5 miles, note another picnic area on the right. The path continues past it. The lake is about 50 to 60 feet below you at this point. As you walk around a finger of the lake, the trail narrows to about a foot in width. On the right, notice the parking area above. Now it's a steep, rocky climb: stay on the main trail through a switchback, ignoring the spur trail to the right.

At about 6 miles, you're at a picnic area and boat ramp. Look for the trailhead sign just past the boat ramp. Take yet another switchback and follow the trail as it roams up and down the hilly terrain. Along here, look for a fairly huge maple tree.

At about 6.5 miles (just past another picnic area) is the path marked Geode Nature Trail. (You'll see several interpretive posts along the nature trail: brochures are available at the park office.) After a few switchbacks along the nature trail, cross a plank bridge that leads to the beach. The bathhouse in front of you has been closed since the mid nineties, but the concession stand opens seasonally. Past the bathhouse is the parking lot with your car. Before you leave the park, stop at the office and check out the park's geode collection.

Overlooks and Vistas

Wildcat Den State Park

Backbone Trail
Backbone State Park

Distance: 1.51 miles

Time: 50 minutes

Path: Dirt, grass. Rock outcroppings on the first 0.5 mile of this path create some tricky footing, so watch your step—although it's tempting to look at the view instead of your feet. After the outcroppings, the path changes to loose, sandy soil (almost like the beach, in several spots).

Directions: From Strawberry Point, go east on State Highway 3 for three miles. Turn south on 140th Avenue (County Road W69). At 120th Street (County Road C57) turn west (right) into the east entrance of the park. About 0.50 mile into the park you'll come to several small parking areas. Park in the lot near the map board. The Backbone Trail is almost directly across the road.

Contact: Backbone State Park, 1347 129th Street, Dundee, IA 52038; (563) 924-2527. www.iowadnr.com/parks

Highlights: Hike along a narrow ridge, the "devil's backbone." The limestone cliffs at Backbone, Iowa's first state park, offer some great views of the Maquoketa River and Backbone Lake. Watch rappellers right from the trail—the bluffs are popular with climbers too. This steeply ridged area, imprinted by the Maquoketa River, was known as "the backbone" even before it became a park and officially received its name.

In the parking area, a map board pinpoints your location. Turn from the map board and face the park road: the Backbone trailhead is across the road on your right. Begin your walk on a tree-lined path with plenty of places to step to the side and look down the sheer cliffs. Before long, the rocky path requires all of your attention. Take a close look at the outcroppings you're navigating around and through: The stones have been etched and shaped into odd angles and patterns. Twisted cedars dot the left edge of the trail.

At about 0.25 mile, you'll come to a popular rappelling area where you can watch rappellers descending the side of the cliff—or awaiting their turn. Look down to the Maquoketa River. On hot summer days, you'll see people splashing in the shallow waters. The path is quite sandy as you begin the actual loop, leaving the rock outcroppings behind. Go straight (south). This loop begins with a short but steep incline. You'll see maple and red oak now, along with the cedar, as the

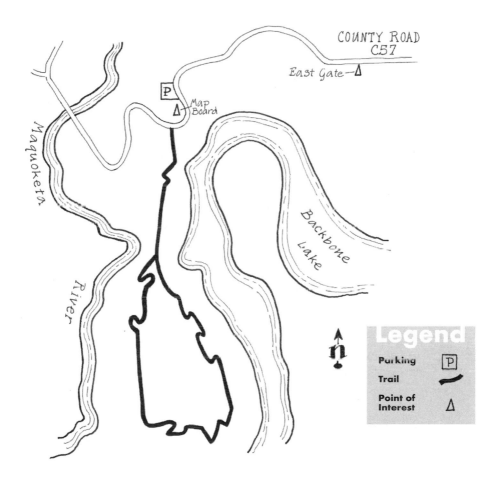

trail widens to about six feet.

In the 1930s, the Civilian Conservation Corps built the dams on the Maquoketa River that created Backbone Lake. To the left, peer down at Backbone Lake, your view nicely framed by sunlit maples. There are several places to leave the trail and look over the edge.

When you've gone about 0.5 mile, you'll see a marshy area, a small pond to your left below. Notice the moss on the trees—and look for tree frogs along here too. At about 0.75 mile, on your left is an open, grassy, low area; on your right is a wooded area. Several faint trails zigzag down to the river. Go ahead and check them out if you wish. Most of these paths dead-end, so be sure to return to the main trail; it's always the higher path. About a mile into your walk, the trail is littered with pine needles. Look up! Several massive white pines tower above your head. Impressive! You might catch a raccoon lumbering along the path at this point too.

**Rock outcroppings along the "devil's backbone"
in Backbone State Park keep things interesting.**

After you reach the beginning of the loop, retrace your steps. Stop and watch the rappellers again on your way back through the rock outcroppings. Take the same short path through the trees and cross the street to the parking area and your car.

Ready for More?

Head over to Backbone Lake's beach to relax—or rent a canoe (check seasonal availability). After a break, you can walk the East Lake Trail near the beach.

East Lake Trail
Backbone State Park

Distance: 3.7 miles (round trip)

Time: 2.5 hours

Path: Dirt, grass. Tree roots and rocks at times make the path more difficult to navigate. Try not to trip while you're watching the wildlife.

Directions: From Strawberry Point go east on State Highway 3 for three miles. Turn south onto 140th Avenue (County Road W69). At 120th Street (County Road C57) turn right (west) into the east entrance of the park. About 0.5 mile into the park you'll come to several small parking areas. Park in the lot near the map board. East Lake Trail is across the road.

Contact: Backbone State Park, 1347 129th Street, Dundee, IA 52038; (563) 924-2527. www.iowadnr.com/parks

Highlights: Sheer rock walls pop in and out of view to delight you. Backbone Lake stays at your right side during the entire walk. You'll see herons taking off from the water, Canada geese, and turtles sunning. Listen for owls too.

From the parking area, look at the map board; it pinpoints your location. As you turn from the map and face the park road, East Lake Trail is across the road on your left. Notice the large shagbark hickory trees as you approach the trailhead. The path starts out sandy with a small amount of rock, then changes to dirt. The six-foot-wide trail follows along Backbone Lake, a long, narrow body of water. Your path is covered with forest litter, including white pine needles; enormous white pines soar into the sky.

Before long, you're directly below a popular scenic overlook on the park road—look up and you might see other walkers waving from above. You also might see a nice patch of late-summer wildflowers here, including black-eyed Susans. Landscaping timbers have been placed in the path to prevent erosion, but the trail still washes out in spots, so watch your step. The path narrows to about two feet at times. Fluffy clouds drifting by are reflected in the lake at your side.

At about 0.25 mile into your walk, you'll reach an impressive limestone bluff (on the left) that towers over the path. A bench fashioned out of stone sits beneath this ledge—courtesy of the Civilian Conservation Corps back in the 1930s. Sit a while and admire the craggy rock formations. As the path curves, you'll come to another sheer rock wall that hangs over the trail path more than the others. It resembles a leaning, oversized pile of boulders that looks as if it should tip over. Moisture drips down from the overhang onto the sandy soil. You'll see another stone bench built by the Civilian Conservation Corps here. Continue on; the cliffs do recede from the path a bit until they are about 25 feet away. (Be sure to stay on the path to avoid poison ivy, which can be abundant along here.) You'll also see some maples, along with basswood and ironwood trees.

At about 0.5 mile, you'll come to a wash that drains downhill. Go across the washed-out area on the path that curves around. Watch tree roots and rocks in the trail along the damp, but not muddy, trail. Now, the cliffs are about 50 feet from the trail. You'll continue to see oaks. Listen for Canada geese on Backbone Lake. Sometimes you can't see the lake, but you can hear the wildlife.

At about 0.75 mile, the rock wall hugs the trail; reach out and touch it. A painted turtle suns on a rock in the glittering lake. As you start an uphill climb, about 1 mile into the walk, you'll cross a plank bridge. Here, goldenrod blooms in the fall, and black-eyed Susans are more than three feet tall. Shortly after this, bear right on the first junction on this trail. Look for the beach in the distance now. The trail is in an open area at this point; in another 100 yards it heads back into a wooded area.

You'll come to another junction at about 1.35 miles. Turn right;

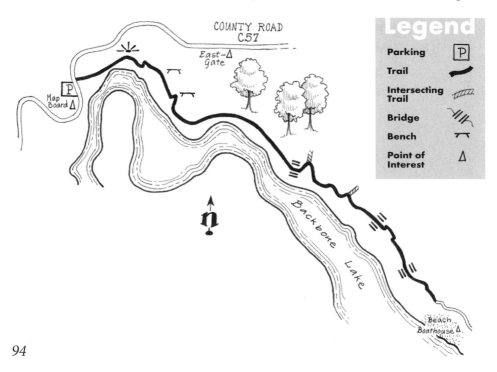

The Civilian Conservation Corps constructed this unique limestone building at Backbone State Park.

continue to follow along the lake. Listen for the deep, throaty voice of the bullfrog. The trail is still sandy in spots—and rocky and damp. At about 1.5 miles, another sheer cliff squeezes in close to the trail. Now, you're on a narrow strip of trail, less than five feet from the edge of the lake on your right—and just as close to the rock wall on your left. Watch and listen for herons on the water; you could see several. The heron's squawk isn't nearly as graceful as its flight over the water.

Listen for the call of a barred owl, especially in the spring and fall. You might hear other owls, too, such as the great horned owl.

Just when you think the trail is getting a little too sedate, more rock formations, one after another, pop into view—a feast for the eyes. Note the crevices on the next cliff—not quite big enough to climb into. Soon you'll cross another bridge, this one about 15 feet long. Around the next corner, the limestone bluffs are in your face again. As you get closer to the beach and the end of East Lake Trail, the outcroppings step back again.

You're getting close to the beach when you can see the dam. (There's also one more small bridge to cross.) Note the presence of the silver maple, a lowland tree that likes it wet. At about 1.75 miles, you'll reach the trailhead. Take off your hiking shoes and sink your toes into the warm sand at the beach. Admire the boathouse while you relax. The attractive limestone structure was built by the Civilian Conservation Corps in the 1930s. Then retrace your steps along the trail, back to the parking area and your car.

Ready for More?
Stop at Bixby State Preserve for a hike to an ice cave. This cool cave is part of an algific slope. The cold air whooshing from the cave feels great on a hot summer day.

Mound Walk
Ocheyedan Mound State Preserve

Distance: Less than 1 mile

Time: 30 minutes

Path: None

Directions: From State Highway 9 in Osceola County, turn south on County Road L58. Take this road through Ocheyedan to the intersection with County Road A22 (also called 170th Street); turn left or east. A sign also directs you. Pay attention once you turn; it's easy to drive past the parking area. The parking area and sign is on your left (east).

Contact: Osceola County Conservation Board, 5945 State Highway 9, Ocheyedan, IA 51354; (712) 758-3709; www.iowadnr.com/preserves

Highlights: You'll be standing tall when you walk to the top of the mound, once considered the highest point in Iowa (now a farm near Sibley is the top dog, with a spot at 1,670 feet). But this hill (a glacial kame) is still impressive—and a favorite landmark, visible for many miles into the countryside.

STATE HIGHWAY 9

Legend

Parking ☐P

Trail

COUNTY ROAD L58

170th St.   (COUNTY ROAD A22)

This informative sign greets visitors to Ocheyedan Mound State Preserve.

Start your walk from the parking area near the mound. A small sign lets you know that horses aren't allowed here; it is a walk-in-only trail. A larger sign, farther on, announces that this is, indeed, Ocheyedan Mound. Although there is not an established trail, a footpath to the top of the mound has been created by the numerous visitors. Along this path, a redwing blackbird may scold as you climb the hill. Note the variety of natural rock in the footpath as you walk along—and the many colors. Look for quartzite and granite.

Check out the views from the top of this glacial kame that was formed thousands of years ago when a glacier melted and heaped layers of sand, gravel, and rock here, forming a hill. It is believed that early settlers used the mound as a landmark. It's easy to understand why, because the mound is visible from quite a distance.

On the northwest side, several large boulders are visible in the grass. Look for brightly colored butterfly milkweed here, along with purple prairie clover and other prairie plants and grasses.

Ocheyedan Mound became a geological preserve in 1984.

Ready for More?
Head to Cayler Prairie State Preserve for a summertime stroll through wildflowers and native prairie grasses.

Pikes Peak Hike
Pikes Peak State Park

Distance: 10.2 miles

Time: 4.5 hours

Path: Boardwalk, dirt, and grass paths. The boardwalk is accessible, within easy reach of the parking area. As you hike other trails, the paths might be soft and grassy, rocky, dry, slick with mud, narrow, or wide. Enjoy a variety of terrains and vistas on these well-marked trails.

Directions: Take U.S. Highway 18 into McGregor. When the highway turns east (left), continue on County Road X56 until you reach Pikes Peak Road (part of the Great River Road), about 1 mile from the edge of town. Turn into the park. You'll see a campground area on the right; veer left. Continue on to the parking lot next to the shelter house, picnic, and concession area.

Contact: Pikes Peak State Park, 15316 Great River Road, McGregor, IA 52157-8558; (563) 873-2341. www.iowadnr.com/parks

Highlights: This park has much to offer: bluffs and valleys, scenic overlooks, a waterfall, Native American effigy mounds, and more. Spend a day here exploring the trails. In autumn, brilliant fall foliage floats above the winding paths. Abundant greenery welcomes you in the summer. In spring, trillium and other woodland flowers reach for the sun in the oak and hickory forest.

Start your hike with a sweeping view of the Mississippi River from one of the two overlooks near the parking area. Arrive just before daybreak and watch the sun break through the fog on the Mississippi. Beautiful! As you leave the overlook, check the map board and pick up a brochure with a map of the trails. (Several kiosks in the park offer trail information.)

From the sidewalk near the shelter house, signs point the way to the Crows Nest, the Bridal Veil Falls, and the Hickory Ridge Mounds. Notice the large shagbark hickory and white oak as you head in a northerly direction toward these sights. About 300 feet into your walk is Bear Mound. This Native American (Woodland Culture) effigy is an example of animal-shaped ceremonial mounds, unique to the upper Mississippi River Valley.

Past Bear Mound, the boardwalk begins beneath a canopy of trees. You'll see maple and basswood here, along with a bench and another observation area. Go down a series of stairs to reach Crows Nest, an

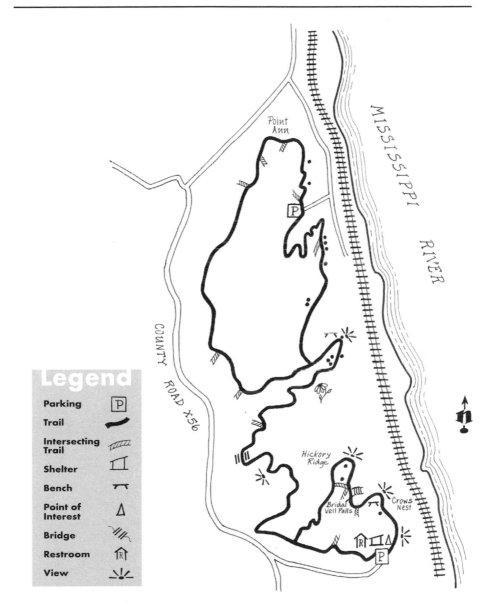

overlook with a view of the river. About 0.25 mile into the walk, you'll come to a couple of boardwalk junctions. Both are well marked—just keep to the right—as you head toward Bridal Veil Falls. Although the falls display isn't expansive, it's a fun stop. You can walk behind the trickling falls after climbing over a few slippery rocks. In winter, as the "sheet of water" freezes, it resembles a bridal veil.

When you're done here, go back up the stairs to the last well-marked intersection.

Now you're headed to the Hickory Ridge Mounds—a straight shot

Enjoy sweeping views of the Mississippi River from the trails at Pikes Peak State Park.

up more stairs. After about 58 steps, stop at the bench and take in the view—you're higher than the falls, looking down into a ravine. After you've climbed all 153 stairs, you'll have hiked about 0.65 mile.

At the top is yet another bench and a junction: keep right. The Hickory Ridge Mounds are in an open grassy area to the left. Continue on; you'll pass by quite a few mounds, including effigy (animal-shaped), conical, and linear. Even with a park map, the mounds can be difficult to spot because they blend easily into the slopes and hills. It's fitting that they are part of the natural beauty here.

At the end of this path is Hickory Ridge Overlook with yet another scenic vista of the Mississippi. Enjoy the view, then walk on the other side of the mounds until you reach the Point Ann trailhead. You've walked about 1 mile now. As you enter the hickory and oak forest at the trailhead sign, notice the ferns—bunches of them. Leaves and forest litter cover much of the four-foot-wide path, even in the summer. The trees are spread out—at least 10 feet apart, giving the woods an airy feeling. When you reach the first junction in the woods, keep right. (A signboard indicates that Point Ann is still 3 miles away.) Here, the dirt path widens a bit. You've hiked about 1.5 miles to this point, some of it uphill.

Now it's downhill. Mosquitoes make their presence known in the low areas (be sure to pack insect repellent). The ravine on your right is a steep drop-off, about 300 feet down from the path's edge. Note the paper birch—easily identified by its white peeling bark. At about 2.25 miles, stop and enjoy the scene before you. Water gurgles over rocks and across the path, disappearing down the ravine. Jumbles of jewelweed sprout up in the moist areas, bright dots of color against a backdrop of lush green. In summer, it's the most serene spot on the trails. You've descended about 113 feet from the first intersection on this trail.

About 2.5 miles into the walk, cross a small bridge over a culvert. Notice the limestone outcropping on the left—and what looks like a bathtub with a long pipe draining into it. (It's actually a cattle trough left over from the days when this area was a farming homestead.) Now you'll head back up; the paths are rocky with natural limestone.

At the next junction, a sign points to the right for Point Ann. (Homestead parking is to the left.) The path changes to grass for a while, then back to dirt and rock. A massive maple hovers over the path. Next, you'll come into a clearing with wild bergamot and Queen Anne's lace blooming in late summer. As you walk, listen to barges on the river below. Scenic spots continue to crop up, one after another. At about 3 miles, you'll encounter a plentiful patch of wildflowers and sumac. Nice! Shortly after this, there is a bench that looks straight down to the river, another scenic vista. Now you can actually see the barges.

You'll come to another junction in another 0.5 mile: turn right. Although the trail to Point Ann is well marked, and the overall trail distances are accurate, the miles en route may be less reliable. Keep in mind how long you've walked as you go along. (A GPS is a fun tool to bring on hikes to track your path and miles.)

When you've hiked nearly 4 miles, there will be another bench. (Ready for a break?) Now, you'll start descending. Pay attention to the footing on this rocky path. Just after a switchback, at the next junction continue straight, still headed to Point Ann. Past this intersection, a bench overlooks the river, yet another scenic spot. Keep descending on a series of switchbacks that wind through mostly wooded areas. The trail is between two ridges at this point. Mosquitoes will hunt you down, so reapply your repellent often!

Listen and watch for woodpeckers on your walk: downy, hairy, or even pileated varieties can be found at Pikes Peak. At a junction with a gravel road, turn left onto the road. (You've hiked almost 5 miles now.) Walk the road to the sign just ahead that marks the McGregor parking area (for people who aren't into hiking, this is the spot to park and then go up to the Point to enjoy the view).

Two trails lead to Point Ann from this parking area. Take the trail to the right; it is the shorter path. And it's uphill from here. Soon you'll hit another switchback. Then you'll need to suck it up for one more steep hill before you reach Point Ann. (You'll climb 200 vertical feet in about 0.25 mile.) At the next junction, go straight. Yes! You're at Point Ann!

With so many lovely vistas along the way, you're a little spoiled by the time you reach Point Ann. The view is nice but not spectacular. Don't hike this trail just to get to Point Ann and the lookout. Hike it for the whole package—the miles of pleasing trails along the way.

On the way back, take a slightly different path (some sections will be the same). After you've guzzled enough water, take the first trail on your right into the woods. (Ignore the spur trail that leads to the McGregor parking area.) In about 0.35 mile, you'll be at a junction. A sign indicates that Homestead Parking is straight ahead—this is the path you want for now. Look at the windmill remnants to the right. The trail flattens here. Keep going straight at the next junction, noting the water reservoir on the right. In late summer, daddy longlegs scurry across the path. Watch for red fox on the way back too.

You'll start a gradual ascent as the trail weaves in and out of woods and through grassy clearings. At about 6 miles, in an open expanse, notice the purple clover, Queen Anne's lace, thistle, and milkweed. Back in the woods a short distance later, the first trees you'll see are red oak. The dirt and grass path has widened to about six or eight feet. Late summer, the buzz of cicadas fills the air. At the next junction, go straight (signs indicate the direction to Pikes Peak). A soft, grassy path lies ahead as far as you can see.

Go left at the next junction (signs still mark the way). It's a pretty, open area with goldenrod, wild raspberries, bergamot, bluebird houses, and bluebirds. At the next intersection, bear right. For the next 2 miles, this section of trail is the same path you took on your way to Point Ann. You've walked about 7 miles to this point. Although this is a wooded area, the grass is so green and plush it looks out of place—like someone's manicured lawn. Now, the path goes uphill.

Shortly after 9 miles, at another junction, go straight. In another 0.5 mile or so, turn right at the intersection and follow the signs back. You'll come out of the woods into the parking lot near the shelter house area. Pat yourself on the back and head to the concession stand for some cold water and a well-deserved snack.

Ready for More?

Stay overnight in the area. (Try a bed and breakfast, small inn or even camp out. But space fills up quickly, so plan ahead.) Then tackle Effigy Mounds National Monument or Yellow River State Forest the next day.

River Ramble
Palisades-Kepler State Park

Distance: 3.4 miles

Time: 2.5 hours

Path: Dirt, a few remnants of gravel/crushed rock, park road. The trail width varies—it might be a foot wide or eight feet wide. There are steep, root-covered segments.

Directions: From Cedar Rapids, take U.S. Highway 30 east (about 12 miles). A sign alerts you to the right turn at the park's entrance. Follow the park road until it dead-ends at a parking area near the river. (Stop at the park office first, if you wish, and pick up a brochure.) Along the way, admire the bluffs and sandbar.

Contact: Palisades-Kepler State Park, 700 Kepler Drive, Mount Vernon, IA 52314; (319) 895-6039. www.iowadnr.com/parks

Highlights: Limestone bluffs and ravines, Indian mounds, and winding paths through woods with river views. In the 1930s, the Civilian Conservation Corps built many of the park's facilities, including roads, hiking paths, and the rustic stone lodge. This is a peaceful walk.

Begin your walk in the parking area near the river. As you face the river, look to the fence on your right (north). A trailhead sign identifies the path as Cedar Cliff Trail. In the spring, patches of sweet william greet you along this eight-foot-wide path. Notice the red cedar along here.

The trail starts out with rock outcroppings. About 200 feet into the walk, turn left at a junction and cross a wooden plank bridge. Listen to the Canadian geese on the river to your left. You'll see more sweet william, violets, wild geranium, snags, and limestone outcroppings as you walk along the shaded path. At the next junction continue on; do not turn right.

Watch out for roots and rocks on the trail (now just a few feet wide). Note the ferns and moss growing from the outcroppings and the occasional red columbine too. If you're hiking in the spring, the wildflower display is wonderful.

The pleasant trail meanders along the river. As you start an ascent at 0.25 mile, glance up—you'll see at a small lookout above you on the trail. At the next junction, continue on the same path. A wooden plank bridge takes you over a gully and to the gazebo and lookout area. What a unique spot! Look at the compass carved in the stone floor of the gazebo. Peer over the log railing at the sheer cliff and the twisted, gnarled red cedars below. Palisades-Kepler is home to one of the oldest trees in Iowa: a red cedar that is more than 450 years old.

Rapellers enjoy the park as well. A sign here reminds them to register at the office before they begin. As you continue on the crushed-rock path, notice the rustic log railing on the left and a foot-high retaining wall on the right. Now there is a mowed clearing and more red cedar.

At about 0.35 mile, the path descends and bends away from the river. You'll encounter a switchback shortly. Enjoy the wild geranium along here. You'll see spring beauty in other spots along the trail. As the trail heads back to the river, stay on the main trail; ignore the footpaths forged by visitors. Now you'll see some maple. The river is below on the left; woods are to the right. Look for maidenhair fern along the paths as well.

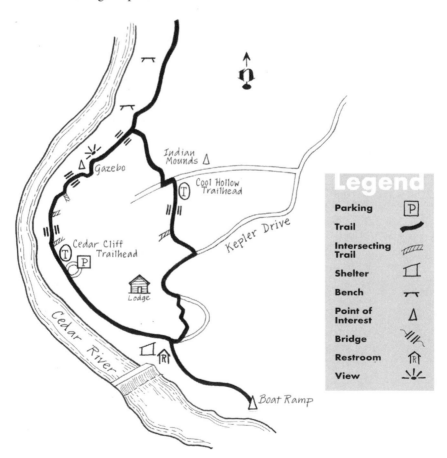

Palisades-Kepler State Park offers up wooded paths with wild-flowers, bluffs, and scenic river views.

If the footing gets tricky as you descend, just hang onto the rock outcroppings for support. At a stone bridge and an intersection, continue on the path; don't turn. Take a break on a bench high above the river and enjoy the views. Notice more twisted red cedar about 50 to 75 feet down.

The rugged trail has tangles of roots to maneuver through (and a sandy soil). The roots actually help with your footing as you start the steep ascent. In the spring, fragrant shooting star blooms nearby. The trail veers to the right as it meanders up and down. You may need to climb over a few downed trees across the path.

After another bench that overlooks the river, you'll start descending again. Notice the large white oak here. Patches of sweet william look like miniature bouquets scattered across the woodland floor. Wild geranium is a constant in the park too. At about a mile, you'll reach the end of this trail; retrace your steps to the junction with the stone bridge. Now take the other trail and turn left. The path is a few feet wide and starts ascending almost immediately. A walking stick would come in handy—it's a huffer. Climb over a few downed trees on the trail. But hey—the trees also make a great place to stop and rest on the way up. Near the top, turn and look at the hill you've climbed. You'll be impressed. In less than 0.25 mile you've climbed about 156 vertical feet.

At 1.65 miles, you'll reach a junction with a road. Turn left, cross the road, and walk along the right side. In a short distance, you'll see the Cool Hollow Trail sign on your right. Take this trail. (The Indian mounds are farther down the same road, under large trees.)

Cool Hollow Trail is only a foot wide, with remnants of crushed rock or gravel. No traffic sounds here. As you walk along, you will descend along a ravine with more downed trees to scramble over. Notice maidenhair fern along here too.

Just short of 2 miles, you'll come to a junction with a bridge; continue straight. As soon as you cross the bridge, you'll start an uphill. Listen to the quiet here, it's awesome. Notice the large maple trees too.

In less than 0.25 mile the trail intersects with a road. Walk this road past the lodge (there is a bit of trail along here too) to a Y-intersection with another park road, then turn left (south). Follow the road toward the dam. (You'll pass a restroom and picnic area on the right.) Although there is a pickup trail near the water, it's just as easy and scenic to walk along the road. Gaze at the bluffs across the river. Dig your toes into the sandbar near the lower dam (if the water level is low). Then retrace your steps to the Y-intersection, bear left (in a northwesterly direction), and follow the road to your car (about 0.35 mile away).

Scenic Overlook Trails
Ledges State Park

Distance: 2 miles

Time: 2 hours

Path: Crushed rock, dirt, boardwalks, and plenty of stairs.

Directions: From State Highway 17 about 10 miles west of Ames, go west on County Road E52 (also 250th Street). (Traveling from the south, you'll see a sign that says Ledges State Park, 3 miles.) At a T-intersection, turn left. Do not enter the park's east entrance. Stay on the hard-surface road past the Lost Lake Nature Trail, a shelter house, and restroom. Park in the lot closest to the one-way park exit.

Contact: Ledges State Park, 1519 250th Street, Madrid, IA 50156; (515) 432-1852. www.iowadnr.com/parks

Highlights: Scenic overlooks, sandstone cliffs, and a creek that spills onto the park road in several places, creating mini-waterways to splash across on lazy summer days. But there's a tradeoff for the scenic vistas. You'll climb up or down more than 1,200 steps on this walk.

The raw beauty of the sandstone bluffs is most apparent in the winter, when bare-boned trees accentuate the bluffs' hard lines and angles—no softness here. In autumn, spectacular color lures hikers. Spring brings budding beauty and a fresh look. Or hike in summer, when the lavish landscape is reward enough for climbing the stairs.

Begin your hike in the parking area at the lower (west) end of the park. Glance at the flood pole notched with flood dates and levels from 1957 to1993. The mark for 1993 is 25.5 feet—that's a lot of water!

From the parking lot, turn right (north) and walk on the road a short distance to the park exit. This one-way road is closed in the winter (on both ends of the park), but you can still access the trails on foot. In summer, vehicles exit here (after meandering through the park from the east entrance).

As you walk into the park past the gate, the bluffs are already starting to rise. See if you can spot any beaver dams on the creek to the right. Around the first curve, notice the rock outcropping. Unfortunately, lots of initials and have been carved into the soft sandstone. Just past the rock outcropping, walk across the grass to the stairs with a wooden railing. The steps go up—and up. Notice the Kentucky coffee tree near the steps. In the fall, its thick brown pods litter the grass.

When you've climbed about 19 stairs, you'll see a Hutton Memorial sign and another set of stairs to the left. Continue on; do not turn left. By the time you reach a multilevel lookout with built-in benches, you'll have climbed 178 stairs. It's a junction as well; take the stairs to the left and continue your ascent to the top of the bluff. After about 64 more steps, past another lookout platform and a switchback, you'll reach the top. You'll have walked about 0.35 mile and climbed more than 300 steps (with an elevation change of about 214 feet from the beginning of the walk). Enjoy the lookouts as you reach them; the views change dramatically with the seasons.

The sharp fragrance of pines will reach you before you can actually see them on top of the bluff. Here, take a short detour to the left, if you like, and stop at the Hutton Memorial Stone, in honor of Murray Lee Hutton, the first director of the Iowa State Conservation Commission in 1935.

Otherwise, at this junction at the top, turn right onto the path that drops down and follows along a slope. Several small footpaths take off

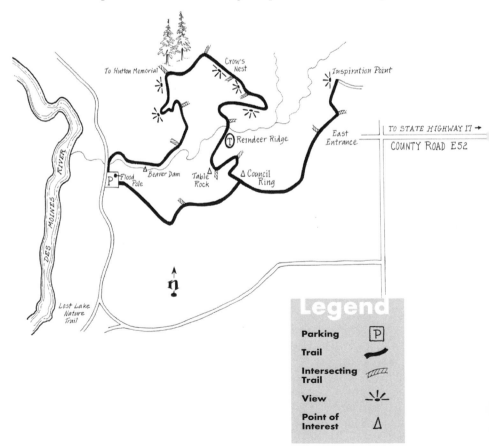

to the left. Ignore them; stay on the established trail as it curves to the right. Notice the basswood trees, along with oak and even some maple, depending on the slope. Here, the path widens to about six feet, with a small amount of crushed rock that doesn't hide the deep indentations from deer and other animals. Soon you'll come to another junction; several grassy paths take off from the main trail into the woods. Ignore them as well and stay to the right. Listen for hawks —you'll likely hear one or two.

Now you'll descend about 44 railroad-tie steps to another lookout platform and bench. In winter, you can easily see the Des Moines River from here. Enjoy the view, then continue your descent, stopping at three more lookout platforms. Stay off the intersecting paths—stick to the main trail. Did you notice that many of the rustic steps along here are simply two or three stones put together? Watch for loose stones beneath a leaf-covered path in autumn. In winter months, ice can be a problem.

Eventually, you'll wind down to a parking and picnic area. The trailhead sign identifies the trails you're exiting as Old Indian Trail and Crow's Nest Overlook. You've descended about 335 stairs in less than 0.25 mile. Study the intriguing sandstone bluff to your right; it looks as if a face has been etched in the stone.

Down the road to the left is a picture-perfect stone footbridge— take a detour and walk across it, or stop near it when you're done hiking. This is a lovely spot for photos, by the way. In the summer, nearby picnic areas will be filled with visitors.

The creek flows over the road here. Hop across the water on the cement blocks on the side of the road to keep your feet dry. (In winter, you might have solid ice to glide across.) Of course, if your hiking boots are waterproof, simply slosh through the water. In warmer months, families wade the shallow creek, snooping for tad-poles, minnows, frogs, and other fun stuff. When it's hot, kids line up near the road, shrieking with delight whenever a car obliges and splashes them.

After crossing the water on the road, look for the Reindeer Ridge and Table Rock Overlook sign. An arrow points the way up to some— yep—more stairs. You've hiked about 0.75 mile to this point. Look at the unique Reindeer Ridge boulder with a reindeer etched into the stone at the trailhead. As you begin ascending the stone steps, ignore several junctions to the left—keep right.

Soon you'll reach a boardwalk. When the boardwalk drops away, watch the unprotected edge—it's a long way down. The path is about three feet wide now, with some crushed rock (the boardwalks are about five feet across). Note the sandstone ledges as you pass by. Does the last one remind you of the underside of a giant mushroom?

As you ascend again, on newer boardwalk stairs, check out the neat

Several winding paths lead to the top of the sandstone cliffs at Ledges State Park.

shelf of rocks, the intricate layers of sandstone exposed. Look for reindeer lichen (it resembles dried-up moss). The ridge was named for this lichen, which is rare to find this far south. After a few more stairs, you'll come to about 61 steep, older stone steps. At the next lookout you're standing on sheer rock that juts out above the creek. A chain-link fence guards the edge. This is Table Rock. The sandstone beneath your feet, unfortunately, has been carved with initials, names, and dates, some weathered, some new. From this vantage point, look across the park—and see where you began your walk.

In winter, rusty-topped oaks cling to remnants of their fall finery, rubbing elbows with leafless, pale sycamores. You'll continue to climb—it's the only way to go.

At the next junction, ignore the trail to the right. This is a switch-back of sorts, and you're walking on a narrow ridge. After a few more stairs, turn right at the next junction. You'll do another switchback—and climb about 50 more stairs. At the top is a large, semicircular area called Council Ring. Here, you can go straight, into the forest, or you can continue along the ridge that leads down to the parking area. Go straight. From the road to the Council Ring, you've climbed about 299 more stairs.

Although the trails are steep (and that's part of the fun), everyone you meet on the paths is having a good time—and their enthusiasm is catching. The trails see a lot of summer activity as families explore the ledges. It's easy to access the trails in so many spots—and the boardwalks are fun for kids of all ages. Visit in winter if you prefer more solitude. The crisp air is invigorating—and no mosquitoes!

As you continue straight into the forest, the path widens again—about six feet or more. Notice shagbark hickory along the level path—a welcome break after the stairs. Eventually the path widens to almost 10 feet, and you'll head downhill. Be sure to check out the views of the canyon along here.

You'll reach a junction on your left now, with a series of steps down to the road. Ignore it. At the next junction, bear left. Here, the trail meets up with the road and Inspiration Point. Look down into the park and enjoy yet another great vista. Do you feel inspired as well? You've walked about 1.25 miles to this point.

Now retrace your steps to the Council Ring. At the junction here, turn left, descending about 129 railroad-tie steps to another junction; turn left. Check out the view at the small platform lookout before you make this turn and continue to descend.

Go down about 134 more stairs to the trailhead, where you'll be able to see the parking lot. Follow the grass path to the lot and your vehicle.

Ready for More?

Pick up a trail map at the east entrance and check out your options. Several trails near this entrance take you through prairie and woods—without the stairs. Or head for the Lost Lake trails. (The lower trail is accessible.) Walk to the river bluff. Can you see the pro-file of an eagle in the rock?

Wildcat Den Walk
Wildcat Den State Park

Distance: 4.25 miles

Time: 2.5 hours

Path: Crushed-rock, dirt path. The path widens and narrows along bluffs and rock outcroppings. Stairs, a boardwalk, and bridges are part of this walk too.

Directions: From Muscatine, travel east on State Highway 22 through Fairport. In about 1 mile, turn left (north) on Wildcat Den Road, which will take you to the old mill, the schoolhouse, and an area where you can park and begin your hike.

Contact: Wildcat Den State Park, 1884 Wildcat Den Road, Muscatine, IA 52761; (563) 263-4337. www.iowadnr.com/parks

Highlights: This walk encompasses oak and hickory bluffs, ravines, and overlooks, stands of huge pine trees, unusual rock outcroppings, and historic buildings. Stop at the Pine Creek Grist Mill, built in 1848 (and listed on the National Register of Historic Places), and the Melpine Schoolhouse.

Begin your walk at the signboard near the parking area and the mill. The signboard tells you about birds (warblers, woodpeckers, indigo buntings, and more) in the area, along with the terrain and landform (Southern Iowa Drift Plain). The trailhead is directly across the road from the schoolhouse and parking area. After you cross the park road, a few wooden steps lead to the marked trailhead. The crushed-rock path is about five feet wide as you enter a canopy of trees. The path goes uphill immediately; you'll climb about 100 feet in less than 0.25 mile before the trail levels off. Notice the abundance of jewelweed. At about 0.35 mile, at the first junction, the path to the left leads to a parking area; go straight here.

Shortly after this is an overlook area. You're above the treetops; below is a jewelweed-covered slope. Nice! The path narrows to three feet now—and in some places it's only a foot wide. At 0.5 mile, notice the huge white pine. Now you're starting a downhill with about 33 stairs. The path continues to go up and down. In another 0.1 mile, you'll descend about 41 more steps to reach a boardwalk over a low area. Wildflowers surround you as far as you can see: jewelweed, hoary vervain, yellow coneflowers. Although this seems like a strange mix for a wooded area, enough light must get through to support the wildflowers. This is a beautiful spot. Enjoy!

When you continue on, the path is only a foot wide, lined by four-feet-tall jewelweed. Soon after this, you'll reach another bridge and an intersection. Cross the bridge, then turn right. (You will return to this spot on the way back and retrace your steps from here back to the parking area.) If you're lucky, you may spot a pileated woodpecker as you ramble along.

At the next junction, continue straight (don't take the trail that goes up on top on the ridge). Admire the 70-foot bluffs towering above as you walk along. Trees growing on the rock overhangs shade the path. Pine Creek is on your right. Notice the water trickling down the bluff on the left. At about 0.75 mile, still walking beneath the cliff, you'll need to maneuver around some large rocks. A path takes you through these large boulders—it's a fun scramble. Notice the seepage

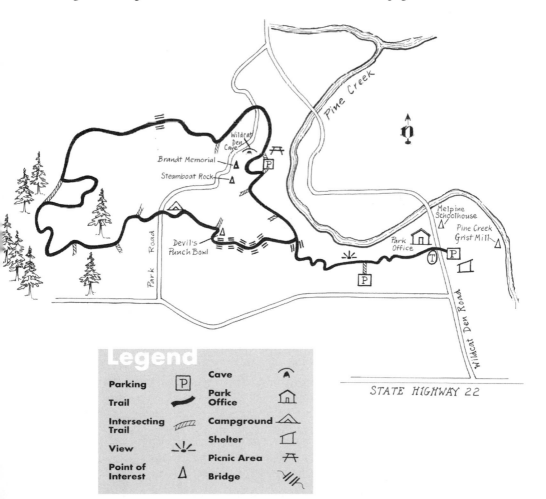

113

of orange-hued water (due to iron) near several outcroppings.

At the next intersection, just past these rocks, go through a wide passageway in the rocks. Unfortunately, here you'll see names carved into the sandstone. Now you'll descend to an area with picnic tables and parking, a nice spot to take a break. You've walked about 1 mile to this point. See if you can spot Steamboat Rock and other fun outcroppings before you continue.

Trails in Wildcat Den State Park wind past dramatic overlooks and unusual rock outcroppings.

When you're ready, climb about 50 stairs that lead to the Brandt Memorial and the dens (you'll see a sign). The memorial honors Emma and Clara Brandt, who donated a portion of the parkland. Then climb around and explore the dens, including Wildcat Den Cave. This is a popular section of the trail; you'll probably encounter a few other hikers checking out the caves. Return to the trail (this doesn't loop back) and continue on. Back on the trail, you'll see the path to the right that heads down to the same picnic and parking area where you were previously (don't take it).

Now leave the bluffs behind as you head uphill to an intersection with a park road at about 1.25 miles. Directly across the road, pick up the marked dirt trail (up a few steps). At the next Y-intersection, turn right. (You've climbed about a hundred feet again.) Watch for deer; they're plentiful along here. If you enjoy the challenge of a steep descent, you're in luck: A toe-jammer is just ahead. Watch your footing as you descend until you reach a bridge that's about 40 feet long. Ready for an uphill climb? You've got it. Now you'll travel the same 100 feet back up. Then the path curves south near a fence, which is a park boundary line. To the right, past the fence, is a field. At a junction of 2 miles, the path goes straight or left. Turn left.

Ah, this is where the pines are. A huge stand of pine unfolds before you. These are (at least) 40-foot-tall pines, rows and rows of them. The quiet envelops you as soon as you reach the plantation; stroll along a path cushioned with pine needles, thick with pine cones. A raccoon may wander by. For the next 0.5 mile, you'll walk in and out of these majestic pines, through a clearing, along a switchback, and then back deep into the pines. This may well be your favorite part of the walk. You'll find jack pine and Scotch pine here.

You've walked about 2.5 miles now. If you're lucky, you may spot a pileated woodpecker as you wander the trails. At the next junction, the path to the right leads to a road (and a church). Go left. Soon there is another junction; be sure to go straight because the path to the left dead-ends. Another junction pops up almost immediately; go left. You are still walking among pine trees, but you can see a field beyond.

At 3 miles, at a Y-intersection, bear left. When you reach a campground road, go straight across the road to pick up the marked trail. Now you've left the pines behind. (Sigh.) The gravel trail is six to eight feet wide. Take about 38 steps down and turn right, heading to Devil's Punch Bowl. You've got a boardwalk and an overlook; look down and see the path you'll be walking on shortly. (This is quite an overlook!) Now take about 82 more steps to a bridge at the base of the Punch Bowl. Enjoy the view here too. This is a low area; ridges rise on both sides of the trail (from the campground road to here, you've descended about 130 feet).

You'll cross four more bridges of various sizes in the next 0.1 mile. Notice the ferns along the trail. At 3.5 miles, you are back to a portion of the trail that you walked at the beginning. Turn right and retrace your steps (slightly more than 0.5 mile) back to the parking area and your car.

Ready for More?

Visit the Nye family cemetery nearby. (Benjamin Nye, one of the first settlers in the area, built the mill.) Many of the stones date back to the 1800s, providing another glimpse into history.

Prairie
Paths

Cayler Prairie Walk
Cayler Prairie State Preserve

Distance: 1.67 miles

Time: 1.25 hours

Path: None. There are no established trails, but several faint footpaths have been created by visitors to the prairie.

Directions: At the intersection of State Highway 86 and State Highway 9 west of Spirit Lake, go west on State Highway 9 for about 3 miles, then make a left turn onto 170th Avenue (County Road M38). This gravel road takes you to the preserve. Look for it on your left side in about 2 miles, just after you pass the intersection with 170th Street. A large sign marks the entrance to the preserve and a small parking area.

Contact: Iowa Department of Natural Resources, Big Sioux Wildlife Unit, 2248 125th Street, Spirit Lake, IA 51360; (712) 336-1485. www.iowadnr.com/preserves

Highlights: Wander in this native prairie on a breezy late summer day and enjoy. The rocky landscape, the knobs, and the low areas were formed by glacial debris thousands of years ago. Wear long pants for your walk.

Begin your walk at the Cayler Prairie State Preserve sign. A plaque set in the ground near the sign tells you that Cayler Prairie has been designated a Registered National Landmark. Although there aren't any established trails, there are a few footpaths to guide you into the prairie, but they soon disappear. In summer, wild roses are sprinkled across the landscape. In July, you'll see leadplant, Queen Anne's lace, coneflowers, and more. Listen for the pheasant's cackle; one might take flight from a patch of grass near you. It's not uncommon to see bobolinks too. Finches add to the melodic nuances of the prairie.

Take the faint footpath to the left and begin a gentle downhill. Look around; you have a nice view of the prairie here. It's also peaceful on the prairie; listen to the wind as it hums through the grasses, the occasional sputter of a car passing by, and the birds. As you start to climb the next knob or hill, the path fades away. Pale purple coneflowers pop up everywhere as you walk the prairie. At the top of the next hill (you've probably walked about 0.5 mile now), you can see a creek and a fence in the distance. This hillside also is covered with pale

You can always count on open spaces and wind humming through prairie grasses at Cayler Prairie State Preserve.

purple coneflowers in summer. Notice the small rock embedded in this hill as well.

As you continue up and down the knobs, pick your path carefully. Some of the lower areas are thick with thistle. Note the variety of ferns. Swamp milkweed blooms on occasion too. The grasses vary, but you'll probably see little bluestem and Indian grass, among others. As you forge ahead with no path, notice several large holes in the ground —perhaps one is a badger's den.

On the next hill, a big boulder rests partway down the incline, a great place to sit and gaze out at the prairie. Wild roses, Queen Anne's

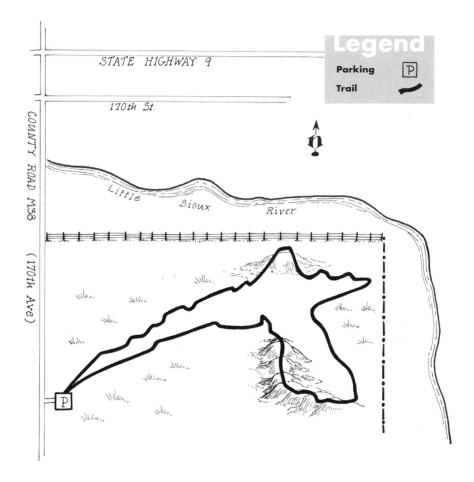

lace, and hoary vervain are all nearby.

Back in a lower area, about 200 yards beyond some fence posts, is a creek or stream (past the creek, the land rises to a hill). Turn around and look at the gentle slopes you walked. You've hiked about 1 mile to this point. Follow the eastern line of hills or knobs and look to the right; there are more low hills to climb.

At about 1.35 miles, you're on top of one of the hills; continue to go up and down as you follow the gentle hills on your way back. You'll have a nice view of the windmills (they are across the road from the prairie) on your return to the front of the preserve. As you head for the parking area, you might hook up with one of the footpaths again.

Ready for More?

Wander as much of the prairie as you wish—there's plenty to explore. Take another hour and add another mile zigzagging across the gentle prairie.

Goat Prairie Walk
Pohlman Prairie Preserve

Distance: 1.01 miles

Time: 35 minutes

Path: Mostly dirt through the wooded area—and none in the prairie (except faint footpaths made by visitors). Although the path starts out about five feet wide, it quickly changes to a few feet wide—or less—with a steep incline along a ravine to the top of a bluff and a patch of prairie.

Directions: From Durango, take U.S. Highway 52/State Highway 3 south. The entrance to the preserve is not marked; watch for it on the left side of the road (just outside of Durango). If you reach Clay Hill Road, you've gone too far. Turn into the gravel parking area, where there is enough room for about five cars.

Contact: Dubuque County Conservation Board/Swiss Valley Nature Center, 13606 Swiss Valley Road, Peosta, IA 52068; (563) 556-6745. www.dubuquecounty.com

Highlights: Have you ever hiked a goat prairie? Now is your chance! (A goat prairie exists on a steep, dry slope and has shallow soil.) The wooded path starts out sedately enough but works into a steep switchback that leads to the top of a limestone bluff—and native prairie remnants. Let your gaze sweep across the Little Maquoketa River Valley, an excellent view.

Begin your walk at the unmarked trailhead adjacent to the parking area to the left (west) of the yellow sign that says Wildlife Management Area/Wildlife Preserve (posted by the red gate). Don't go behind the red gate—it's not the trail.

As you begin your walk on the five-feet-wide grassy trail, it changes to dirt and narrows to a few feet in width. Note the ravine to the left and a slope on your right. You'll start an uphill climb in just a few hundred yards. Maples are common along here; you'll also see some white oaks. Watch for roots along the trail too.

At 0.1 mile, rock outcroppings appear on the right; to the left is a steep drop-off. Listen to the quiet here as you head to the top of the bluff, but keep your eyes on the foot-wide trail (which also is moss-covered at times).

At about 0.2 mile, a switchback takes you down and across a ravine. The path sharply veers left (straight ahead is a barbed-wire fence). Although the ravine may be dry during your hike, the wash

121

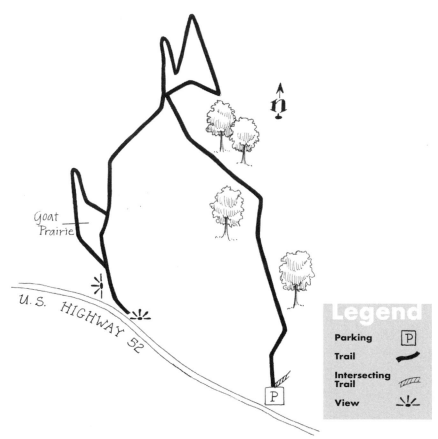

Goat
Prairie

U.S. HIGHWAY 52

Legend

Parking	P
Trail	
Intersecting Trail	
View	

could fill with runoff after a heavy rain.

Now, the muddy path is a mere six inches wide in some spots. Mayapples past their prime pop up occasionally in the summer. Watch your footing on the steep switchback: deer tracks that end with a slide are visible on the path.

Once you reach the bluff top, check what's blooming in the goat prairie. In summer, leadplant blooms. Prairie grasses to look for include sideoats grama, little bluestem and big bluestem, and prairie dropseed. A semblance of a trail has been forged by other visitors. Follow this faint footpath to the edge and look out over the Little Maquoketa River Valley. A few red cedars up here offer shade if you want to admire the view for a while. Or wander the prairie some more, then retrace your steps to the parking area.

Ready for More?
Swiss Valley Nature Preserve near Dubuque offers a variety of trails, from forest to prairie to wetland. The interpretive center is worth a stop too.

Juniper Hill and Prairie Trails
Fossil and Prairie Park

Distance: 1.79 miles

Time: 1 hour

Path: Wide grassy paths (about five feet wide) and some gravel.

Directions: From West Maine Avenue in Rockford, turn left onto SW 8th Street (a sign tells you that the park is 1 mile away). SW 8th Street is now County Road T18. At the intersection of T18 and County Road B47, continue on B47 (also 215th Street). You will see a sign for the Fossil and Prairie Park before you turn into the driveway on your right. Park near the picnic shelter.

Contact: Floyd County Conservation Board, 1227 215th Street, P.O. Box 495, Rockford, IA 50468; (641) 756-3490. www.floydcoia.org

Highlights: Native prairie and fossils—all in one park! After your walk, search for a few fossils. Watch for Baltimore orioles as well as bobolinks. The park contains both native and restored prairie. Don't miss the creeping juniper found on Juniper Hill (rare to find in Iowa). Turtles sunning, orioles singing, prairie plants, and well-marked paths make this a fun walk.

Before you begin, stop at the map board near the picnic shelter. Great information here! Get a quick overview of how to search for fossils and the types of fossils you might find, along with a map of the trails. (This area was covered by ancient seas in the past, and the fossils reflect this.)

If you still have questions, stop by the center before you walk the trails. Check out the Devonian fossil exhibit, brightly colored living coral, animal skins, and lots of prairie information.

From the picnic shelter, take the gravel path to the intersection, where you can pick up different trails. Turn left at the sign that says Prairie Trail/Juniper Hill Trail. Almost immediately, you'll make a right turn at an intersection near a wooden fence rail.

Now the path changes to a mowed-grass trail about five feet wide. Rock has been added to the path in several low spots. Watch for the different types of prairie: dry, mesic, and wet (dry on hilltops and sides of hills, wet in bottomland). A Baltimore oriole is easy to spot on the open prairie. As you stroll downhill, look to the right at the unfolding pastoral scene—nice!

At the next junction, turn right, in a northerly direction. (It's the beginning of a loop, so either right or left would work.) This is a low spot, and a section of the trail might be closed after heavy rains. Notice that birdhouses have been placed by the barbed-wire boundary fence on your right.

Now you'll start an incline: Look for herons, egrets, and a variety of migrating waterfowl on or near the pond to your left. Walk down to the small building near the water; it's open for bird observation. Notice the willow and cottonwood growing near the pond. At the top of the hill, look back down at the pond and the pastures beyond—it looks like a patchwork quilt. About 0.5 mile into the walk, the trail shoots off to the left or straight. (If you turned left, you'd cut through the middle of the loop—a shortcut.) Don't take it—continue straight. Now you are climbing Juniper Hill! Turn around and look at the scene

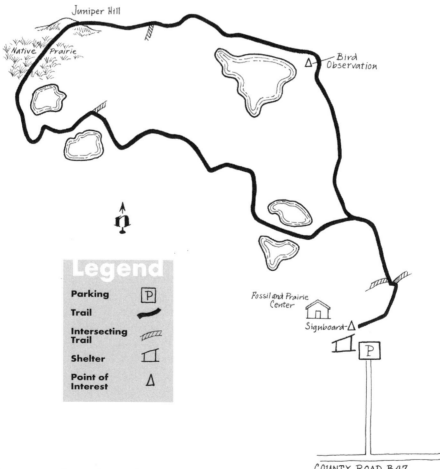

below as you climb. In another 0.25 mile, you are at the top. The creeping juniper (fenced off) is a rare plant in Iowa—this may be one of the few places you'll find it growing in Iowa—although it's common in Canada.

Here you'll also find goldenrod, wild grape, and some milkweed. Although a prairie blooms from spring to frost, the types of plants that are in full bloom vary throughout the summer. Visit often, and watch the layers of a prairie unfold. Other flowers you'll find in the park include pale purple coneflower, blazing stars, and butterfly milkweed.

The park has more than 60 acres of native prairie. As you walk these paths, look for prairie dropseed, sideoats grama, and other grasses. You may spot a bobolink on your walk as well!

At about 1 mile, notice the pond to the left, about 100 yards off the path. You'll see ferns along here. In a few steps you'll reach another junction; turn right (this is the other side of the shortcut through the middle of the loop that you didn't take).

Now you'll be walking downhill into an area with some trees (at about 1.25 miles). Cottonwoods line up on the left; the trail is muddy through here. In a few minutes, you'll be walking across the grassy dam of another pond on the right. A Canada goose and her goslings march out of the pond. Turtles sun on logs, plopping into the water as you approach.

Before long, at about 1.5 miles, another junction marks the end of the loop: turn right. Now you are retracing steps back to the signboard and pavilion area. Or cut across the path to the center and look at all the displays.

Ready for More?

Take the trails that lead past the fossil quarry, historic kilns, and the Winnebago River—into the town of Rockford. Be sure to dig for fossils before you leave the park!

Overlook and Tallgrass Trails
Neal Smith National Wildlife Refuge

Distance: 2.22 miles

Time: 1 hour

Path: Asphalt and paved trail. This is an easy stroll along prairie paths.

Directions: From Des Moines, head east on State Highway 163 to the Prairie City exit (watch for signs to the refuge). At the exit, turn west onto Pacific Street, the road that leads into the refuge. Continue to follow the signs to the Prairie Learning Center.

Contact: Neal Smith National Wildlife Refuge, Prairie Learning Center, P.O. Box 399, Prairie City, IA 50228; (515) 994-3400. midwest.fws.gov/ nealsmith

Highlights: A tallgrass prairie in all its splendor. Stop at the Prairie Learning Center before you begin your walk for brochures, maps, and other information to help you appreciate this prairie path and other walks at the refuge. Glimpses of buffalo along the way are a bonus. Visit the prairie at midsummer to enjoy a multilayered palette of color and wildlife.

Begin your walk at the interpretive signs east of the Prairie Learning Center. The signs offer trail information and an overview of the prairie (which is mostly restored). You are on the paved, accessible Overlook Trail for the first part of the walk. At the first junction in a few hundred feet, veer to the left (still on the Overlook Trail). This walk is a loop, so you could go either way. Signboards on this section of the trail tell you about the past and the present on the prairie.

At the next junction, turn left onto the Tallgrass Trail as it heads downhill. Swallows and goldfinches are nearby. Look for wild roses in summer; listen for mourning doves. Here, you may be able to see the bison on a hill to the north. Wooden benches mark stopping points along the way. Signboards tell you what you'll find at these "stations" along the trail (as do the brochures from the Prairie Learning Center). You'll see plenty of redwing blackbirds in the low area. Bird calls sound throughout the prairie, creating a medley of voices: staccato chirps, shrill notes, and soft coos. Look up and see turkey vultures high in the sky. Hawks, doves, warblers, and finches are drawn to this habitat.

In about 0.50 mile, you're near the bison enclosure at the bottom of the hill. The tall, woven-wire fence is a giveaway. Several benches are provided for watching the buffalo, if you happen to spot the woolly beasts. (In winter, take the auto tour that winds thorough their habitat. On occasion, the bison have been known to lick the salt off vehicles.) The refuge also has elk.

The trail curves east now; you'll start a gradual uphill as the path pulls away from the buffalo area. You might notice dogwood and some brushy trees now, as well as milkweed and possibly a few American elms. Listen to the wind moving through the grass; it's a nice sound on a hot July afternoon. Yellow coneflowers bob in the breeze. As the prairie is restored and replanted, you might notice mowed or brushy areas. The prairie is a work in progress.

At about 1.5 miles into the walk, you'll reach an overlook and bench. Here, you can see the road that enters the refuge. The pinks and purples of the wildflowers really pop out in mid- to late summer —more color for the prairie's palette. Queen Anne's lace pokes out above the other plants, adding a lacy crown to the prairie. Look for big bluestem too.

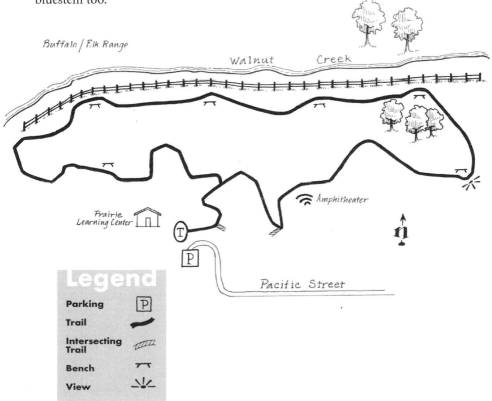

At about 1.75 miles, you'll pass by the amphitheater. Circular rows of benches face the road; enjoy another overlook. Just past the amphitheater you'll hook up with the Overlook Trail again. (At this junction, either left or right will complete the loop and take you back near the Prairie Learning Center and the beginning of your walk.) Veer right for one last scenic overview of the prairie loop you just walked. It's also a chance to catch a glimpse of the buffalo one last time.

Stay on the Overlook Trail and return to the signboards near the Prairie Learning Center. Stop for a visit at the center or continue on to the parking lot and your car.

Ready for More?

Walk the Savanna Trail just down the road (take your car). It's a quick 10-minute walk through restored savanna. Pheasants, wild turkeys, wild raspberries, and a couple of benches make this a short but pleasant walk.

Prairie and Wetland Trails
Lime Creek Conservation Area

Distance: 3 miles

Time: 1.25 hours

Path: Mowed grass. Wide, well-marked trail. Even after a rain, these 10- to 15-foot-wide paths are a pleasure to walk—muddy spots are almost nonexistent.

Directions: From U.S. Highway 65 just north of Mason City, turn east into the entrance to the Lime Creek Conservation Area on Nature Center Road. (Although the address is Lime Creek Road, the street sign says Nature Center Road.) The parking lot is about 1.25 miles down this road on your left. Lime Creek Nature Center is on the right.

Contact: Cerro Gordo County Conservation Board, 3501 Lime Creek Road, Mason City, IA 50401; (641) 423-5309. www.co.cerro-gordo.ia.us

Highlights: Lime Creek provides a variety of habitats for hiking. The restored prairie paths are fun to walk early mornings in the summer—you'll spot bluebirds out catching bugs near their houses. The wetland area can be hopping with leopard frogs. All the trails are easy to access—one loop leads to another.

Stop at the nature center for a trail map and a peek at the wildlife displays before you begin. Examples of prairie plants here can help with identification on a walk. If the center isn't open, take a look at the map board near the building.

From the parking lot, look north to the stand of red cedar, to an opening and a sign that says "Prairie Loop and North Trails." Take this short path (just a few steps) that leads directly to the Red-Tailed Hawk Loop—and the beginning of your walk. Two signs mark the loop: a sign with the shape of a bluebird (this trail is one of three bluebird trails) and a sign featuring a red-tailed hawk. Turn right (east) onto the loop. In about 50 yards, the trail turns left (north). Along this stretch, note the windbreak demonstration and signs that identify various trees, including red cedar, gray dogwood, and hazelnut.

Bluebird houses, placed two-by-two (to reduce competition from other birds), are scattered across the prairie. In June, there may be about six pairs of bluebirds in residence. Deer feed along the paths; it's not unusual to spot a half-dozen of them, silhouetted in the early morning light.

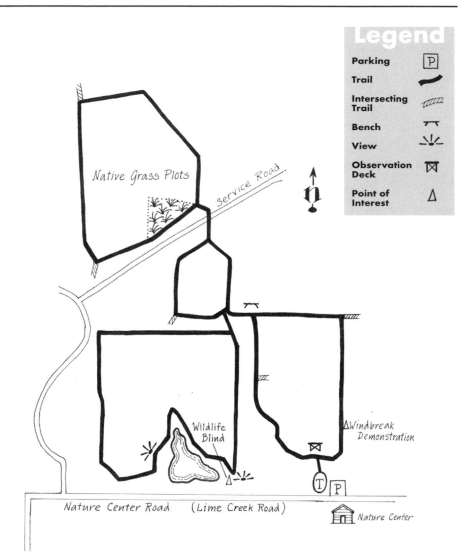

When you've walked about 0.25 mile (just past a food plot) turn left (west). A trail to the right leads to the Badlands Loop—ignore it. Listen for woodpeckers drumming in the mature stand of trees on the right. In winter, without the foliage, it's easy to spot a downy or red-headed woodpecker—or a flicker that hasn't left yet. When you reach a bench, sit for a few minutes and listen to the wind moving through the grasses: big bluestem, sideoats grama, switchgrass. Late autumn, the grasses turn golden, glowing in sunsets. Little bluestem and Indian grass are common sights on the prairie trails.

Just past this bench, at about 0.5 mile, a connecting path leads to the Gray Fox and White-Tail loops. Take this trail to the Gray Fox Loop. In summer, goldenrod, milkweed, and yellow coneflowers follow the gentle bend to the left. Take a right at the next junction. Red cedars hug both sides of the path now. Soon this path will intersect with a gravel access road. Look across the road to the Barred Owl Loop sign (and a bluebird sign). Cross the road and bear right on this loop.

A Native Grass Plots signboard greets you at the beginning of this loop. (The actual signs for the grasses are farther along, on the south edge.) Notice where the various seed plots begin and end. These seeds are harvested in August and September, and some are used for road-side plantings. In July and August, the butterfly milkweed's bright orange blooms add a splash of bold color to the prairie. When you've walked about 1 mile, you'll come to another junction, marked by a large bur oak tree. Follow the bluebird sign and turn left (south), staying on Barred Owl Loop. In the fall, you'll see sumac changing color. At the next junction turn left (east). Here, you'll see the signs that identify the grasses in the native seed plots: little bluestem, sideoats grama, switchgrass, and big bluestem.

Restored prairie paths loop through the Lime Creek Conservation Area.

When you finish this loop, you're back at the intersection with the access road. Cross it to Gray Fox Loop, then turn right and take the section of trail that you haven't walked yet. Cottonwood trees line up along the path, a row of red cedar behind them. There's an abundance of wild raspberries here in summer. Just around the next curve (at about 1.5 miles) is Scotch pine.

At the next junction, turn right onto White-Tail Loop. This area was a pasture for years and is still dominated by cool-season and non-native grasses. (Native prairie plantings may come in the future.) You'll see a line of mature oaks on a quiet slope. Goldfinches perch on tall thistle; dragonflies flit by. By now, you should be feeling quite mellow! At about 1.75 miles, the trail curves left (south). A woven-wire fence is at your side. As you walk up a slight hill, notice the big slabs of limestone embedded in the path—a dozen or so. Once you reach the top of this small hillside (about 2 miles), stop and take a look! Grasses rustle and a patch of pale purple coneflowers sways in the breeze. The pleasant grass path meanders downhill; listen for meadowlarks and finches.

Next, the trail curves into a restored wetland. Watch for leopard frogs springing from the path—be careful not to step on one! Stop at the wildlife blind by the pond. From the bench inside, you'll have a perfect view of the waterfowl, maybe a heron or wood duck. After the blind, go north to finish White-Tail Loop.

When you've walked about 2.5 miles, turn right and leave this loop (on the connecting path), back to the first loop of your walk—Red-Tailed Hawk. A stand of red cedar and Scotch pine will be on your right. You might catch a glimpse of a saw-whet owl. These friendly little owls have been seen in the area, and they aren't shy. Watch for red-tailed hawks too; you're most likely to spot them in spring and fall.

To finish the loop, curve left (east) back to the Red-Tailed Hawk sign where your walk began. Stop at the butterfly garden and wander over to the observation platform for a last look at the prairie. Then take the same short path through the red cedars—back to the parking lot.

Ready for More?

Explore the other trails too—you'll find limestone bluffs, woods, and more wetlands. The Brewery Loop at Lime Creek takes you to the Old Brewery remains. Built in 1873, it is part of the area's history.

Sand Prairie Stroll
Marietta Sand Prairie Preserve

Distance: 1 mile (or whatever distance you choose to walk)

Time: 1 hour

Path: None. Because there isn't an actual path, you're free to wander the prairie. At first you might be preoccupied with watching your feet, trying not to trample the grasses and blooms. Soon you'll discover that this sandy oasis is as resilient as it is beautiful. Birds, butterflies, bees—the prairie hums with life.

Directions: On County Road E29 between Marshalltown and Nevada, turn north onto Knapp Road at the corner near the Hartland Friends Church. The preserve is about 1.2 miles north on this gravel road. Marietta Sand Prairie Preserve is to the east—you can't miss it. Park in front of the preserve; the entrance is near the large wooden sign.

Contact: Marshall County Conservation Board, 2349 233rd Street, Marshalltown, IA 50158; (641) 752-5490. www.iowadnr.com/preserves

Highlights: Never walked a sand prairie? Then this is a great choice for a midsummer stroll! Interpretive signs placed across the upland part of the prairie help identify the grasses and blooming plants. Wear long pants for this walk.

During the summer, the Marshall County Conservation Board places interpretive signs on this native sand prairie, highlighting a variety of prairie plants. Before you visit, call ahead to inquire if the signs are in place—meandering from sign to sign is a great way to view the 17-acre sand prairie. You won't miss out on any of the unique aspects of the preserve, and it's a fun way to learn more about the prairie.

A faint footpath is visible as you enter the prairie, but it fades out in a few hundred feet. Stay in the prairie upland, where the interpretive signs are scattered. You'll see switchgrass, big bluestem, and sand lovegrass. Color starts to settle into the prairie in summer and flourishes by fall. Visit in early August, when the prairie is dotted with bright yellow blooms as the partridge pea sprawls across the upland—a spectacular sight. Stroll among flowering spurge, wild bergamot, hoary vervain, prairie blazing star, black-eyed Susans, and more. Listen for the meadowlark.

The loose, sandy soil (pick some up) might look like sandbox

In late summer, waves of blooming prairie plants cover the Marietta Sand Prairie Preserve.

sand—but it's softer. Walk along the front (west) edges of the preserve too. Note the silver maples at the southwest border—and a lonely red cedar in the middle of the prairie. In the future, more than 200 acres may be added to the preserve.

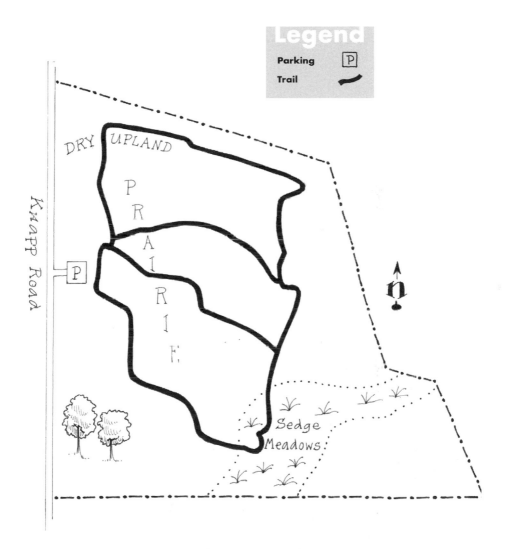

Sedge meadows in the back of the preserve (east) are past a dense stand of aspen. Several deer paths are visible along the southeast side. Unless you're wearing waterproof boots, stay in the prairie upland where the interpretive signs are scattered. (If you decide to visit the wetland, check to see how much rain has fallen in the area.) A bench placed near the entrance is the perfect spot for contemplating the prairie after your walk.

Ready for More?
Each sand prairie has its own personality. Visit the Cedar Hills Sand Prairie near Cedar Falls in Black Hawk County.

Rail Trails and No-Hill Hikes

Old Stone Arch Hike
Old Stone Arch Nature Trail

Distance:	7.66 miles (round trip)
Time:	3.5 hours
Path:	Asphalt. Near the wetland, rock is used. Except for a hill at the beginning of the walk, the path is mostly level, characteristic of a rail trail.
Directions:	From Interstate 80 in far western Iowa, get off at Shelby (Exit 34). As you exit the ramp for westbound traffic, look for the Iowa Agriculture Symbol—a 76-feet-high steel sculpture to the west. Park at the Agri-Symbol Park (next to Tony & Dave's Auto Service).
Contact:	City of Shelby, 419 East Street, P.O. Box 186, Shelby, IA 51570; (712) 544-2404. www.shelbyia.com
Highlights:	This rail trail is easy to access and fun to walk. Hike near a wetland, a train depot, and a city park; across a historic bridge, and through the scenic countryside. Although the trail (round trip) is more than 7 miles, the mostly level path is a breeze to walk.

Begin your walk at the trailhead in Agri-Symbol Park. Sign the visitor's log and pick up an interpretive brochure that highlights the numbered stops along the walk—and also relates some history of the bridge and area.

Although most of the trail is flat, the first 0.5 mile of the trail does contain a downhill that takes you near a wetland area. After a heavy rain the section of trail near the wetland may be flooded. But no problem: If it's wet, just take off your shoes, roll up your pants, and wade through. (Otherwise, you can start the walk near the city park and depot.) Notice the windmill near the wetland. Look for tadpoles and crawdads; frogs will serenade you later in the season. Killdeer race-walk on the path ahead of you. After this, you'll begin to see lots of wildflowers along the path: pale purple coneflower, black-eyed Susan, hoary vervain, and more.

As the path curves north, the flowers continue, especially the pale purple coneflower. Listen to the birds. Enjoy the trail as it roams through the countryside. Notice the catalpa trees' frilly white blossoms (the brochure mentions these trees). Look for the trees just before an intersection with a gravel east-west road.

When you've gone about a mile, cross this east-west gravel road and continue on. At each road intersection, a red gate has been placed on the path, wide enough to let hikers and bikers through while discouraging vehicles. You'll see cattails off to the right and left: This is still a low area. Listen for a pheasant's cackle. The trail here is about 10 feet in width. You'll reach the Shelby Rock Island Depot at about 1.5 miles into your walk. (This isn't the original Shelby depot but is being restored in its image.) Plans are in the works for the depot to open as a visitor center and museum in the future. A Burlington Northern caboose rests next to the depot. This is another trailhead with parking and brochures available as well. The city park is to the left.

Past the city park, cross a paved road (Center Street) and also pass by the Shelby Saddle Club and a small white building, with a sign that says, "Welcome to Stone Arch Nature Trail. Take only pictures leave only footprints." Then cross another road called Spring Street at about 1.75 miles into the walk.

**The Old Stone Arch Nature Trail takes you across a bridge
listed on the National Register of Historic Places.**

Although there are trees along the way, you won't ever see a canopy of trees. Look for some cottonwood or basswood along here, as well as wild grape. Look for hoary vervain and other prairie plants. Beautiful views of the surrounding farmland and countryside accompany you for the rest of the walk. An indigo bunting might flit by. Nice!

At about 2.75 miles, you'll reach the Old Stone Arch. Although the view from the top doesn't do justice to the bridge, you can still appreciate its history. This unique stone arch bridge was built in 1868, using limestone from an Iowa quarry. Such stone arches were uncommon.

Today, it is on the National Register of Historic Places (under the name, "Chicago, Rock Island and Pacific Railroad Stone Arch Viaduct"). Just before a junction with a road is the Stone Arch Airfield. If you're into model airplanes, this is the place to fly them. This is another access point for the trail; brochures are placed here too.

Continue to enjoy the pastoral scenes as you walk. During the summer, black-eyed Susans are abundant along the trail. At about 3.25 miles, you'll see some patches of restored prairie. Look for pale purple coneflower here and prairie grasses. The next mile passes by quickly. Farmers' fields stretch across the landscape, right up to the path now. Notice the terraced fields, which help combat erosion. The sculpted lines and patterns of the fields create a mosaic that rivals any painting you might find in an art gallery.

At almost 4 miles, you'll cross a bridge over Silver Creek. This bridge was created from two bridges that were considered the oldest bridges in the county. Once you cross the bridge, the trail ends at Pingel Timber. There is a picnic table here, so take a break. Enjoy your peaceful surroundings (the land was donated by the Pingel family) and the sounds of wildlife in the stand of trees. Then retrace your steps to Agri-Symbol Park and your car. On the trail, take advantage of the well-placed benches for a few more moments of contemplation before your peaceful sojourn ends.

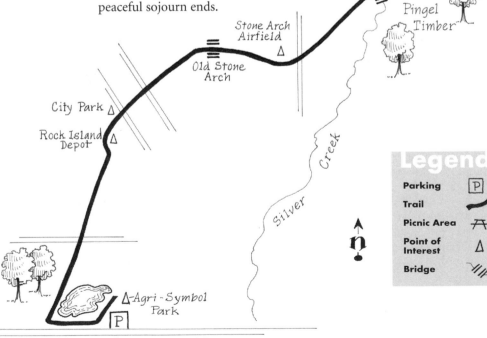

Stone Arch
Airfield

Old Stone
Arch

Pingel
Timber

City Park

Rock Island
Depot

Silver Creek

Legend

Parking   P

Trail

Picnic Area

Point of
Interest

Bridge

Agri-Symbol
Park

P

Puddle Jumper Trail
Orange City to Alton

Distance: 4.13 miles (round trip)

Time: 1.8 hours

Path: Crushed rock. The level, crushed-rock path is about eight feet wide. Jump on the trail in Orange City or Alton: both accesses are well marked.

Directions: From State Highway 10 in Orange City, turn south onto County Road K64, also called Albany Avenue SE. The Puddle Jumper Trail access is about one block from this intersection. Turn left into a circular drive.

Contact: Parks and Recreation, City Hall, 125 Central Avenue SE, Orange City, IA 51041; (712) 707-4885.

Highlights: A level path takes you into the countryside between two small towns. This rail trail is great to walk when you don't have time to hike to a more remote location—yet still want to feel away from it all. Enjoy the exercise stations along the way, a unique feature of this trail. Even the name of the trail is fun! Visit during the Tulip Festival in May and help celebrate the town's Dutch heritage.

B egin your walk from the parking area at the trailhead. A bridle path runs along the north side of the trail for equestrians, a nice touch. As the path moves into the open countryside, notice silver maple, pasture, and farmland on the right. In about 0.5 mile you'll reach a small picnic area. Water break, anyone? Wild roses, black-eyed Susans, and butterfly milkweed make an appearance along here in the summer (and there's sumac too).

Soon you'll pass by the first of several exercise stations. (Each stop has a piece of equipment for a specific exercise/movement—this one has rings.) You've probably never walked a path that has exercise breaks—it's a fun idea.

Then cross a wooden plank bridge at about 1 mile. Shortly after this is another picnic area. A large sign on the open shelter indicates that it is the Depot on the Puddle Jumper Trail. This is a trail access as well. Notice the children's play gym and restroom. From here, cross the gravel road that intersects the trail. A trail sign across the road points the way.

Now the area is more wooded; the crushed rock thins out a bit. Another exercise station is coming up, this one with parallel bars. Try

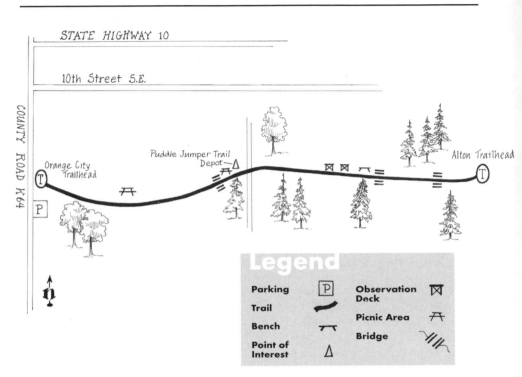

it out, if you wish.

The countryside takes center stage: corn fills the fields on both sides during growing season. Although the distance between the two towns is slightly more that 2 miles, the openness makes you feel as if you are far away from it all. There's talk about extending the trail to the Sandy Hollow Recreation Area and then on to Sioux Center.

The planted pine and spruce trees, including white pine and blue spruce, add a nice touch to the trail. Ready for the next exercise station? This one features a chin-up bar. One, two, three . . . keep going!

At about 1.35 miles, a lookout stand appears on the left (south) side of the trail; it simply overlooks a field. At one time, there were buffalo to gawk at, but no more. Pass by another lookout stand, a bench, and another wooden plank bridge, about 25 feet in length. Notice the scattered silver maples along here and a few willows.

At about 1.75 miles, cross another bridge. Houses are popping up on the right, so you know you're getting close to the Alton trailhead and your turnaround. The planted pine and spruce trees add a nice touch to the trail.

In just over 2 miles, you'll reach the Alton trailhead and another picnic area. A Puddle Jumper sign is posted at this end of the trail as well.

Retrace your steps back to the parking area and your car. You'll enjoy the trail on the way back too.

Sac and Fox Trail
Sac and Fox National Recreation Trail

Distance: 8.34 miles

Time: 3.75 hours

Path: Crushed limestone. This level trail is a pleasure to hike. It's as flat as a rail to trail—and has plenty of shade.

Directions: East of Cedar Rapids, travel on State Highway 13 (also U.S. Highway 151). Look for the Indian Creek Nature Center sign; turn west onto Bertram Road. Just past the Indian Creek Nature Center and Otis Road is the parking lot for the trail. You'll spot the Sac and Fox map board and trailhead sign as soon as you pull in.

Contact: Cedar Rapids Parks Department, 3601 42nd Street NE, Cedar Rapids, IA 52402; (319) 286-5760. www.cedar-rapids.org/parks/walktrail.asp

Highlights: The Sac and Fox is Iowa's first national recreation trail. Enjoy easy access, wide trails, and an abundance of wildlife.

Before you begin, check out the signboard and the map board at the edge of the parking lot. The entire trail is about 7.5 miles (one way). Here, you're at a trailhead near the midway point (next to the Indian Creek Nature Center).

Enter the trail by the map board. Almost immediately you'll cross a bridge. At a junction, the Sac and Fox Trail heads left and right. Turn right. (The Cedar Greenbelt Trail is straight ahead—a wood-chip, hiking-only path.) Here, you'll find another sign board along the crushed-rock trail. Notice the box elder trees as you walk along.

You'll pass by several junctions with the Cedar Greenbelt on your left. Garlic mustard is a nuisance here. Although its white blossoms look pleasant enough, this invader crowds out other woodland flowers and has begun to do so here.

Notice the sweet williams and violets in the spring. Indian Creek is on your right as you amble along this scenic path. At about 0.5 mile, you'll pass beneath a bridge. Shortly after this is another intersection. Bear right; the spur trail to the left leads to a parking/access area. Red-headed woodpeckers are easy to spot along the trail.

Now walk beneath an underpass and then over another bridge that spans Indian Creek. After the bridge, the trail veers sharply to the left. (Now Indian Creek is to your left.) The creek is a constant companion on your stroll.

After a curve to the left, you'll reach a gate that marks an intersection with the road. You've hiked about 1 mile to this point. Although the garlic mustard has invaded a lot of space, you'll still see sweet william and wild geranium too. Wild turkeys may scuttle across your path several times. Deer are abundant!

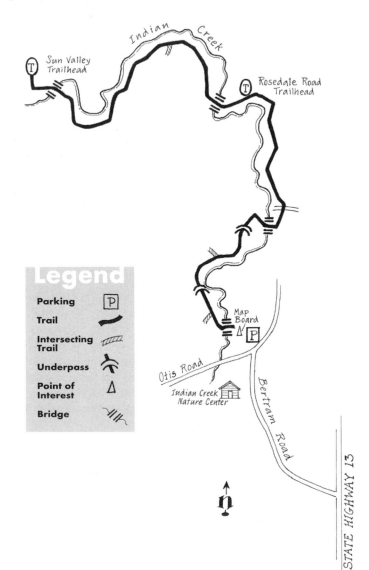

Legend

Parking	P
Trail	
Intersecting Trail	
Underpass	
Point of Interest	Δ
Bridge	

Watch for wild turkeys along the Sac and Fox Trail, Iowa's first national recreation trail.

At about 2 miles into the walk, you're at another intersection with a road. Pick up the path on the other side of the road, which is the Rosedale Road Trailhead. (Pick up a map here too if you wish.) A gate keeps out vehicles. Horses must use the low-water crossing to continue on. At about 2.25 miles, you'll reach a long wooden plank bridge. Cross the bridge and take a break on the bench near the creek. Now the path veers sharply to the right. (Indian Creek is on your right.) Look at the pastureland to your left. Notice willow trees bending toward the trail, and you'll see skunk cabbage unfolding in the spring. You'll also see more garlic mustard, unfortunately.

At about 2.75 miles, you'll reach a junction to the left; continue straight and enjoy the still-level trail. You will likely meet several hikers and bikers out on the trail too. When you've hiked about 3.5 miles, cross another bridge. (The creek is on your left.). Just past the cement underpass, you'll reach the Sun Valley Trailhead. This is your turnaround point. You've strolled slightly more than 4 miles to this point.

Ready for More?
Cedar Greenbelt Trail is right here too. Access these hiking-only trails near the Indian Creek Nature Center. Visit the center too.

145

Sauk Rail Trail
Maple River to Breda

Distance:	14.04 miles (round trip)
Time:	5.6 hours
Path:	Crushed limestone rock. This is a fun rail trail in wide-open spaces. You'll cross 12 bridges between Maple River and Breda.
Directions:	In the small community of Maple River (about 5 miles northwest of Carroll), head north on County Road N20 (Ivy Avenue). Turn right onto Main Street. You'll see the trailhead on your left just past the railroad tracks. Park near the trailhead.
Contact:	Carroll County Conservation Department, 22811 Swan Lake Drive, Carroll, IA 51401; (712) 792-4614. Sac County Conservation Board, 2970 280th Street, Sac City, IA 50583; (712) 662-4530. www.saccounty.org
Highlights:	This trail takes you through the countryside from one small town to another. The old railroad depot in Breda is a nice turnaround point. Or have someone drop your car off at Breda, then walk one way and cut your miles in half. Taking a rail trail is nice when you're not in the mood for any terrain surprises. But it's still a challenge to hike 14 miles, no matter how sedate, so allow plenty of time. Admire the green fields and pastoral scenes along the way.

Park near the trailhead and begin your walk in a northwesterly direction on the wide, crushed-limestone path. Cool spring days are best for this hike. (In summer, biting flies can be an annoyance.) Be sure to bring a backpack on this hike and pack plenty of water and sunscreen. There are no places to stop and get refills between Maple River and Breda.

As you begin walking, almost immediately you'll cross a wooden plank bridge. A sign tells you this is the Sauk Bluebird Trail. You'll appreciate the trail's name as you notice quite a few bluebird boxes lined up along the path. But then you realize that swallows have taken up residence in these boxes.

Enjoy the scenery, the patterns and textures of the fields, the rolling pastureland, and the gentle hills. At about 0.75 mile, you'll reach a junction with a gravel road; pick up the trail on the other side. Here, a sign says this is the Boundary Natural Resource Area. You'll see a couple of willows and a red cedar near this junction. Although the trail is flat, the surrounding terrain is not. At times, the trail is lower than the surrounding countryside.

Soon you'll cross another wooden plank bridge, about 50 feet long. At about 1.5 miles, you'll come to an intersection with another gravel road; cross it and continue on the trail. As you gaze down the trail, note the row of bluebird houses as far as you can see. At almost 2 miles, cross another bridge. Watch for goldfinches flitting by. You've

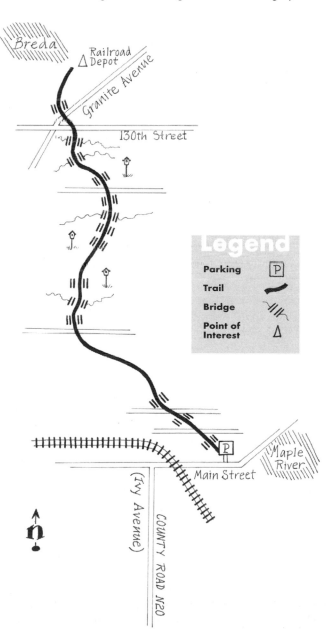

Breda

Railroad
△ Depot

Granite Avenue

130th Street

Legend

Parking	P
Trail	
Bridge	
Point of Interest	△

P
Main Street

Maple River

(Ivy Avenue)

COUNTY ROAD N20

n

gone by 20 or more bluebird houses. At about 2.5 miles, you'll reach an intersection with another gravel road. After crossing it, notice another Boundary Natural Resource Area sign.

Now the path continues on in a more northerly direction, with a slight uphill. As you continue to admire the patterns, the swirls and texture of the planted fields, it's nice to know that the beauty isn't only aesthetic. Contour farming, using terraces and grass buffers, not only creates these interesting mosaics but also has a practical purpose—to help combat erosion on these slopes and hills.

Now cross another bridge; this one is shorter. Red-winged black-birds scold when you get too close. If you're lucky, you might spot a couple of rose-breasted grosbeaks. Trees are definitely not a signifi-cant shade factor on this walk.

On the road, to your left, notice a Hazelbrush Watershed Project sign. (It's not on the trail though.) You'll also see a few red cedar trees.

The next bridge is placed over a swiftly moving creek. Soon you'll see lots of red cedar in varying sizes. By now, you've passed by nearly 25 bluebird houses—with nary a bluebird in sight. Another bridge comes up almost immediately; you've gone about 3 miles now. Signs posted along the way keep you informed about the miles to go.

Now you'll have a slight uphill—and some trees: silver maple and red cedar, along with sumac and a few flowers. It's possible to see Balti-more orioles too. Although the line of trees along the path is sparse, look to the right; the hillside is thick with red cedar. If you're keeping track of bluebird houses, you've gone by about 38 boxes.

After you cross yet another bridge, watch for more birds, including the bobolink. The next bridge passes over a babbling brook at about 4 miles into the walk. Now the trees fade away, and you're back to scenic pastoral views again and more bluebird boxes. A sign reminds you that this is the Sauk Bluebird Trail.

At about 4.5 miles, you're at an intersection with a gravel road; cross it and continue on. Notice the red cedar along the trail and another wooden plank bridge coming up. Gently rolling hills sur-round you, sloping down to the trail. Although the terrain is not flat, your path stays level and easy to walk (a rail trail characteristic that you'll appreciate). Now a few trees provide some momentary shade, so this is a good spot to dump the rocks out of your shoes. The crushed rock is easy to walk, but those small pieces have a way of sneaking into your shoes (and take a water break while you're at it). You've walked past about 75 bluebird houses now.

Look at the huge cottonwood here, about 50 feet in height. Farmers' terraced fields are on both sides of the trail. This part of the trail has been carved out of the hills, so you can't see above them for now. After another bridge, you'll see more silver maples and several cottonwood trees. Now there is a field to your left, a hill to the right, and another bridge.

At about 5.75 miles, cross 130th Street and stay on the trail. As the trail curves left, in about 50 yards it will intersect with Granite Avenue. Cross Granite Avenue and pick up the trail on the other side. Go over the last bridge on the way to Breda at about 6 miles. Still counting bluebird boxes? You should be up to about 90 houses at this point.

As you get closer to the town of Breda, notice some planted pines. At 7 miles, you're in Breda! Cross the main street in town and walk to the picturesque old railroad depot. A sign lets you know that Maple River is slightly more than 7 miles away. The signboard tells you that more than 700 bluebird boxes have been placed on the Sauk Rail Trail from Swan Lake State Park to Blackhawk State Park. Although you saw about a hundred of these houses, unfortunately, there didn't seem to be many bluebirds enjoying the boxes. Despite volunteers' efforts, swallows and other birds have nabbed more than their fair share of real estate along the trail.

At the depot, take a break on one of the benches outside. If you brought lunch in your backpack, bon appetit!

Lean back against the bench, close your eyes, and imagine the excitement of waiting for the train at a new depot in the early 1900s. You can almost hear the train whistle and the faint echo of family goodbyes that must have taken place here. Although the depot is open to the public by appointment only, look inside: a potbelly stove, old crank phone, telegraph, and gas lantern are scattered across the small room, remnants of the past.

Stop at the nearby convenience store for a snack and bottled water before you head back to Maple River and your car. The hike back may take slightly longer because you've already walked 7 miles, and you may not be quite as fresh.

Summerset Trail
Carlisle to Indianola

Distance: 11 miles (one way)

Time: 4.5 hours

Path: Asphalt. The miles quickly go by on a beautiful spring, summer, or fall morning. This level rail trail is a good choice when hiking conditions might not be so great elsewhere (like during a wet spring).

Directions: From State Highway 5 in Carlisle, turn west onto 165th Place. The trailhead is clearly marked and visible from the road. Turn into the gravel parking area, where there is an information board. Because this is a one-way hike, have someone drop you off at the Carlisle trailhead. Your pick-up point will be at the Indianola trailhead on North 5th Street. (Or have someone leave a car for you at the Indianola trailhead.) Of course, the hike is just as pleasant if you choose to begin in Indianola and reverse the walk.

Contact: Warren County Conservation Board, 15565 118th Avenue, Indianola, IA 50125-9005; (515) 961-6169. www.warrenccb.org

Highlights: There is great birding on this trail, so bring your binoculars! This hike is teeming with wildflowers, birds, and waterfowl. Plus, you'll cross about 20 bridges (which includes the spots where there are bridge-type railings, but no wooden planks to walk across). The trail is popular for biking, jogging, and walking, but chances are you will only meet a few other people along the way.

At the trailhead on the edge of town, take a look at the "Welcome to Carlisle" information. A trail map is posted along with area information. The wide asphalt trail leads you right into the countryside. You'll cross the first wooden plank bridge (bridge #1) about 900 feet into the walk. Listen to pheasants cackling nearby; watch for bluebirds. It's apparent from the very beginning that this will be a great birding walk.

The trail runs parallel to 165th Place for now. Shortly into the walk, you'll pass by a marshy area with cattails; listen to the frogs humming. In about 0.75 mile, cross over another wooden plank bridge (bridge #2), just past a housing development entrance. Now you'll see farmers' fields on the right. Also notice the large cottonwoods, rows of them—and wild roses too. Look for spiderwort in late spring and early summer. Bluebird houses can be spotted along here as well.

Now pass by the Heggen Farm and an intersection with Clark

Street. The parallel road, 165th Place, turns into Dubuque Place and becomes gravel. If you need a break, there is a bench at about 1.75 miles, followed by another wooden plank bridge (bridge #3) over a drainage ditch. Here meadowlarks sing, and red-winged blackbirds scold as you pass close to their nests in this grassy open area.

At about 2 miles, you'll cross another bridge (bridge #4) of sorts (just railings, no wooden planks to walk across). To the right (west-southwest) is a pond with Canada geese and other ducks. Honey locust trees grow in this low area (look for the thorns, an easy way to identify them), as well as more cottonwood. At 2.5 miles, the trail intersects with 158th Avenue. You'll see more ponds and wetland areas, and maybe a great blue heron. You may notice some teals on a pond too.

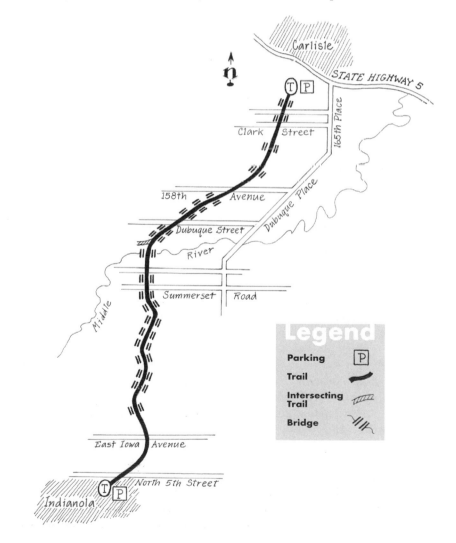

When you've walked about 2.65 miles, cross another bridge (bridge #5)—this one has a small stream beneath it. Farmers' fields on your right may have standing water in wet weather. Notice willows along here and more bluebird houses. Wild roses keep cropping up here and there. By this time, you should have a rhythm going with your stride; if not, well, what are you waiting for?

Just past another bridge (bridge #6), you'll see some tall cottonwoods stretching to the sky, at about 3 miles. Wild grape makes an appearance, too, along with more honey locust, elm, and patches of wild roses. When you've gone about 3.35 miles, cross a bridge (bridge #7).

Ah, the birds. You'll likely see several Baltimore orioles and Eastern goldfinches (the Iowa state bird). Notice the silver maple along the path, common in a lowland area. At about 3.75 miles into the walk, Dubuque Place intersects with Dubuque Street, which you will cross. Then, in about 15 feet, you'll cross yet another bridge (bridge #8). This one is about 50 feet long, with a pond below that spreads out on both sides of the bridge. Take a moment to look around and appreciate how scenic and serene it is here. Farmers' fields stretch out before you, dotted with barns in the distance, and the road that paralleled the path has disappeared. Silver maples line up along here too.

As you walk, notice another pond to the left. Meadowlarks and finches are still plentiful. You'll come to a fairly large pond at about 4.5 miles on the right. In another 0.25 mile, cross a bridge (bridge #9) with a small creek running beneath it.

Soon after this, you'll pass by a short connecting path (on your right) that leads directly into Iowa's newest state park: Banner Lakes at Summerset State Park. (The right side of the road is a designated bike lane that loops through the park.)

Stay on the asphalt Summerset Trail. The trail has been going in more of a westerly direction; now it bends back to the south. Birds flit by, darting from one side of the trail to the other. Look at the huge cottonwood trees, maybe 40 feet high. Watch for rose-breasted grosbeaks along the trail, always fun to spot.

At about 5.25 miles, you'll go over one of the longer bridges (bridge #10); this one has a woven-wire railing, and it crosses over Middle River. In another 0.25 mile, the trail intersects with a road to the left. Notice Virginia waterleaf along here.

At 5.5 miles into the trail, you'll come to another bridge (bridge #11) over a stream; there is some erosion going on here. Soon you'll have a bench and an intersection with Summerset Road (a hard-surface road). Woodpeckers are common along here. Red columbine makes an appearance, along with other woodland flowers on this shady part of the walk.

At about 6 miles, cross a bridge (bridge #12). Here, you'll see the delicate pink and purple colors of wild geranium and more huge cottonwoods on the right. Notice thrushes along the trail here too. At 6.5 miles, cross another bridge (bridge #13) with a creek beneath it. Now the trees have faded away, but more bridges are coming up. You'll cross six more bridges in the next mile (bridges #14-19). Keep your eyes open for a pair of Baltimore orioles. A bobolink might show up, too, as you walk beside rolling pastures and farmers' fields. Pheasants cackle nearby. On a sunny spring day, the miles pass by almost effortlessly.

At 8.5 miles, notice the red gates on either side of the trail—and another small bridge (bridge #20, the last one!). Next is an intersection with a hard-surface road, American Concrete on the left, and the Indianola water tower to the right.

When you've walked about 10 miles, you will cross several city streets—just stay on the trail. The pastoral scenes have been left behind as you pass a co-op, metal buildings, and some old cars.

At 11 miles, you'll reach the Indianola trailhead as it intersects with North 5th Street. This is your pick-up location, or where you dropped off your car earlier. The trailhead has a new parking lot, restroom, and a drinking fountain—a great place to end this walk. A sign says McVay Trail. Across the street, the trail is now called McVay Trail.

Ready for More?

Take a stroll on a scenic loop through Banner Lakes at Summerset State Park—Iowa's newest state park. The park can be accessed from the Summerset Trail. Or take U.S. Highway 65/69, north of Indianola, to the park entrance.

Springs, Wetlands, and Waterfalls

Pilot Knob Recreation Area

Bog and Tower Hike
Pilot Knob State Park and
Pilot Knob Recreation Area

Distance: 6.42 miles

Time: 3.75 hours (or more, if the paths are wet and muddy)

Path: Dirt, gravel/rock, and mowed grass. The trails within the park are well marked. When you enter the Pilot Knob Recreation Area, the multiuse trails are rugged and soggy (with mud) for about 1 mile. Weatherproof hiking boots are best for this part of the walk.

Directions: From State Highway 9 east of Forest City, turn south on 220th Avenue. Then turn west on 340th Street and continue to the park's east entrance. Follow the park road to the parking area near the observation tower.

Contact: Pilot Knob State Park, 2148 340th Street, Forest City, IA 50436; (641) 581-4835. www.iowadnr.com/parks

Highlights: Climb to the top of the Observation Tower and enjoy the view from one of the highest elevations in Iowa. Then wander past Dead Man's Lake, an imaginative name for a sphagnum bog—the only one in Iowa. Seek out your own favorite spots for wild raspberries and gooseberries. This walk takes you into the recreation area too—with some scenic surprises.

From the parking area enter the trail on your right, taking the short path that leads to the Observation Tower, an inspiring way to start your walk. The tower is listed on the National Register of Historic Places, along with other structures within the park.

The gravel, six-foot-wide trail quickly changes to dirt. You'll see logs placed on the ground to combat erosion. It's a quick uphill, with oaks shading your path. Climb about 48 metal steps to the top of the tower, which was built in the 1930s by the Civilian Conservation Corps. Although you're high in the sky, at 1,450 feet, the official high spot in Iowa is Hawkeye Point, situated on a private farm near Sibley.

Look out across farmers' fields, the countryside dotted with windmills, and Forest City. Imagine pioneers, as they traveled west, using the knob as a guide for their journey. When you've gawked long enough, retrace your steps back to the parking lot. You've walked about 0.5 mile now. Pick up the trail on the other side of the parking area (by a trailhead sign.) The four-foot-wide dirt path, with some gravel near the beginning, has washed out in spots. Notice the moss on the path and trees.

Turn left at the first junction on this trail. The trail narrows (it's only about a foot wide now) and follows alongside Pilot Knob Lake. This path tends to be muddy and slick, so watch your step. You'll see some basswood and plenty of deer and other animal tracks in the mud. At about 0.65 mile, notice the small clearing close to the lake, a great spot for taking photos or gazing out over the water (on the right). To this point, you've gone slightly downhill. Now you'll be ascending to a more rugged path above the lake. Pick some wild raspberries in July. Listen for mallard ducks on the lake. At the next junction (about 1 mile into the walk), turn right. Take a break on the bench here if you wish.

Now you're at Dead Man's Lake (on the left). This unique, four-acre sphagnum bog is a kettle that formed when glaciers melted in Iowa thousands of years ago (it's the only one in Iowa). Notice the lilies floating on the surface. Stay on the path that curves around the bog, ignoring the next two junctions. You'll see some red oak and maple on the bog side and even some white oak. The path wanders from the bog's edge along here. Soon the trail is grass. Notice the willow, a lowland tree, along with an abundance of wild grape and wild raspberries. When you enter a wooded area again, the grass is

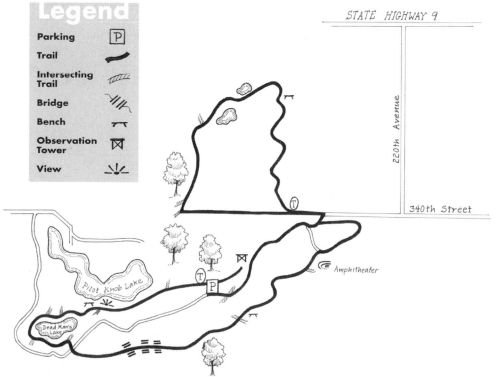

gone. Early spring, before budding trees block the sun, snow trillium and Dutchman's breeches poke out of the ground.

Continue to go straight at the next junction—but take a look down the trail to the right. You'll see a shelter house, picnic tables, a grill, and a restroom. If you wish, take a break here, then return to the same path. You might meet other hikers picking gooseberries and raspberries by the bucketful in season.

The Pilot Knob Recreation Area (adjacent to Pilot Knob State Park) offers plenty of wide-open space for hiking.

You'll come to another junction at about 1.5 miles into the walk. At this point, you can finish your bog loop and go back past the lake, or you can turn right and head for the amphitheater trail. Go right, up about 20 steps to the road. Across the road is a signboard; this is where you'll pick up the trail. (The sign says it's another 1.5 miles to the amphitheater.)

This section of trail begins with gravel. Although the actual path narrows and widens, at times to only a foot in width, it is well cleared on the sides for about 12 feet. Note basswood and red oak along here. At about 2 miles, there are three small stone bridges to cross (over drainage pipes and a culvert). Listen to blue jays jabber along the trail's gentle ups and downs. The next juncture at 2.5 miles is a four-way intersection. The signboard points out that the intersecting multiuse trail is for equestrians too. Continue on the trail marked for hiking. The narrow dirt path morphs into a wide grassy path with mature trees, including oaks. Listen for a pheasant's cackle and its sudden flight.

At 3 miles, you're at another junction. The amphitheater is to the right (it's also on the National Register of Historic Places). Take a detour and check it out if you wish. Otherwise, continue on the same path, up an incline to a picnic area. Now you're on a loop on the park road near the east entrance. Turn right and follow the loop to the entrance. Just outside the park entrance, turn left (facing the road) toward a sign that marks the trailhead to the Pilot Knob Recreation Area.

The rugged, downhill path ahead is challenging. Deep mud, water pooled in horses' hoof prints, and large rocks will slow your progress as you deliberate each footfall. Weatherproof hiking boots are a must for these multiuse trails, particularly after a rain. (If you'd like to by-pass this section of the walk, return to the park loop and follow the road back to the parking area near the Observation Tower—and your car.)

In just a few minutes, turn right at a junction. The mud here gets worse, and you're probably wondering if it's better to bail out now— or hope for the best. With each step, your footprint fills with water. There is no escaping the mud. Finally, in about 0.5 mile, the trail transforms into a grassy path—whew!—leaving the "swamp" behind.

You'll see aspen along here. And there's a bench, which is just the place to take a break. Grab a stick and scrape the mud off your boots. The beautiful grassy path widens to a 15-foot wide swath that stretches across the landscape as far as you can see. If you make it through the mud, you'll fall in love with this grassy oasis. White clover covers the path. Soon the path leads you between two ponds, with the larger pond to the left. Red-winged blackbirds fuss at your approach, leopard frogs make an appearance, and a doe drinks deeply from the pond. Ah, this is more like it. Stop and soak up the serenity.

Notice the willows and a lone cottonwood as you walk. At the next junction, about 4.5 miles into your walk, go straight. (The path to the right leads to a parking area.) Too soon, the scenic haven ends—and you'll head back into the woods. In about 0.5 mile, turn left at a junction. Another intersection pops up immediately; turn left again. Although the path is muddy, it's nothing compared to the "swamp."

At 5.5 miles into the walk, continue straight at another intersection (to the left is the loop you just completed). In another 0.25 mile, you'll leave the recreation area and return to the park entrance. Don't get back on the trails though. Instead, follow the winding park road, lined with oaks, back to the Observation Tower parking area and your car.

Ready for More?

Explore the trails at Lime Creek Conservation Area (about 26 miles from Pilot Knob). Pick from prairie loops, wetlands, woods, and river walks. You'll find limestone bluffs too.

Malanaphy Springs Stroll
Malanaphy Springs State Preserve

Distance: 2.14 miles

Time: 1.25 hours

Path: Dirt, some gravel. The wide trail leads directly to the falls.

Directions: From Highway 52 on the north side of Decorah, turn left onto Pole Line Road (also known as County Road W20). Stay on this road for several miles, until you reach Bluffton Road; turn right. Watch for a small sign on the right side of the road just before you turn into the limited parking area for Malanaphy Springs.

Contact: Iowa Department of Natural Resources, Upper Iowa Wildlife Unit, 2296 Oil Well Road, Decorah, IA; (563) 382-4895. www.iowadnr.com /preserves

Highlights: Walk 1 mile to a beautiful spring and waterfall. This preserve also contains algific talus slopes (cold air from ice below ground seeps up, which creates an unusual microclimate) and scenic bluffs. Scramble up the path at the side of the waterfall for a unique perspective of the preserve.

The trail is adjacent to the gravel parking area that only holds a few cars. A gate at the trailhead lets you know that the wide path is for foot traffic only. This gravel and dirt path is about six feet wide—and surrounded by sugar maple trees. Woodland flowers add to the beauty of the area. Look for wild geranium in the summer, as well as Virginia waterleaf, sweet william, violets, and ferns.

As you start uphill, the path narrows. Enjoy the rock outcroppings and their unusual shapes. At 0.25 mile into your walk, look to the left; down below is the Upper Iowa River, a nice view. There are quite a few snags among the trees. It's wet along here, and moss grows on the tree trunks.

This is a lush, beautiful walk. Although the cliffs rise sharply, your path does not—for the moment, at least. But be sure to stay on the trail. Algific talus slopes are fragile and can be damaged if walked on.

The trail goes up and down a bit now, and you'll notice rocks on the path. Huge ferns hug the path—and the trail narrows to about a foot. At times, you'll need to climb over a fallen tree limb or smaller branches on this natural path. Look for a flash of color from a scarlet tanager, one of the most striking birds to spot.

At about 0.75 mile, you will start going uphill again. When you've

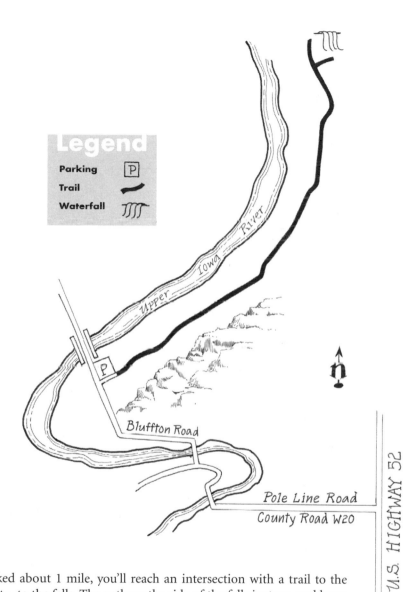

Legend

Parking   P

Trail

Waterfall

Upper Iowa River

P

Bluffton Road

Pole Line Road

County Road W20

U.S. HIGHWAY 52

walked about 1 mile, you'll reach an intersection with a trail to the right—to the falls. The path up the side of the falls is steep, and loose rock inhibits your progress, so step carefully. A walking stick or walking poles would come in handy here. Near the top of the falls are crevices to explore. It's fun to see the water shooting out from the cliff and tumbling down, creating a lovely, misty waterfall.

Ready for More?
Head over to Dunning's Spring Park in Decorah for another great waterfall and more miles of trails.

Marsh, Lake, and Woodland Walk
Kettleson Hogsback Wildlife Management Area

Distance: 2.26 miles

Time: 1.25 hours

Path: Dirt and grassy areas. The smooth trail includes a few inclines, but it's a nice, easy walk with a marsh, lakes, and wildlife to enjoy.

Directions: From the town of Spirit Lake, take Peoria Avenue north to County Road M49, and continue north. From M49, turn west onto 125th Street, which takes you to the entrance of the wildlife management area. Follow the entrance road as it curves past the DNR office and several maintenance sheds; turn right. This short gravel lane takes you to a turnaround loop and trailhead.

Contact: Iowa Department of Natural Resources, Kettleson Hogsback Wildlife Management Area, 2248 125th Street, Spirit Lake, IA 51360; (712) 336-1485. www.iowadnr.com

Highlights: This walk takes you up on Hogsback Ridge, through the woods and near the water. Watch for wood ducks, Canada geese, and other wildlife.

Start your walk at a turnaround and trailhead northeast of the Department of Natural Resources (DNR) office. (Pick up a map at the office if you wish.) The wide trail starts off with some gravel and then changes to dirt. West Hottes Lake is on your left as you stroll beneath oaks. Turn left at the first junction. Now you have a lake on both sides; Marble Lake is on your right. West Hottes Lake is actually a large marsh. Canada geese can be seen here and throughout the area.

At the next junction, you can go left or right. A lower trail takes you closer to the lake. Stay on the upper trail and go straight.

As you walk along on this narrow strip of land between two lakes, you are on top of Hogsback Ridge. This ridge is a glacial remnant. As the two lakes on either side formed from melting ice, debris built up, creating the ridge. The land is about 15 to 20 feet in width here, and there is a 30-foot drop-off on each side.

At the next junction, you'll see a post with an arrow. One trail heads off to the right (and hooks up with the lower trail mentioned earlier). Continue straight. Just beyond this junction is yet another intersection. Here, turn right. (The trail to the left dead-ends after a downhill.)

In spring, notice violets blooming in the forest litter. Soon, you'll see East Hottes Lake to the north. The path continues to be an easy, level trail. Now you'll have a slight descent just before a junction with a trail on the right. Stay on the main trail. Notice a marshy area to the left; listen to the chorus of frogs. You're now closer to Marble Lake (on your right). Look for more Canada geese. Notice the wood duck houses along here; wood ducks are often seen along the lakeshore.

Continue straight at yet another junction. Marble Lake is still on your right. The trail, you'll notice, alternates from grass to dirt as you walk. The path may be 6 to 10 feet in width or a narrow trail. Grass—then dirt—then grass again.

At the next junction, continue to follow the path near the shoreline. At this point, you'll see woods on the left; Marble Lake is still on your right.

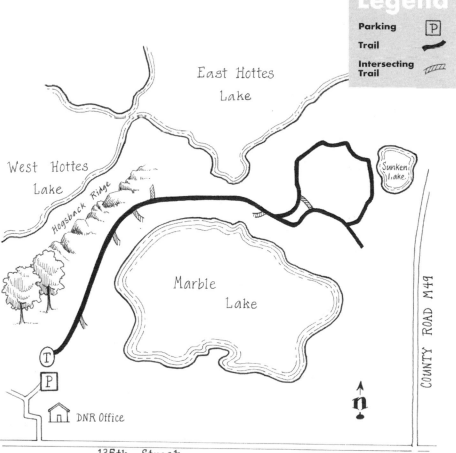

At the next junction (to the left), go straight. Notice the cattails along the lakeshore. In about 0.5 mile, you'll reach another parking area and a junction with a gravel road. A gate across the trail here identifies this as a wildlife management area. Now retrace your steps to the last intersection; turn right. You are turning away from Marble Lake now. As you walk the incline, listen to the Canada geese. Sunken Lake (a very small lake) is on your right. This incline takes you to higher ground on a small ridge. Look east beyond Sunken Lake and you can see a larger body of water (farther away) that is called Spirit Lake.

Although Sunken Lake is small, there is a lot of activity. Here, or on one of the other lakes, you might see blue-winged teals, coots, and wood ducks.

The dirt path is gently rolling as it curves toward a low area. You've gone about 1.25 miles to this point. Soon you're passing by the same marshy area with the wood duck houses and plenty of frogs (but on the other side of the marsh). As you finish this small loop turn right at the junction (in a westerly direction). Take another right almost immediately. Now you're back on the original trail.

Retrace your steps back to the trailhead. If you didn't notice on the way out—pay attention now. You have three lakes in view: East Hottes, West Hottes, and Marble. Back at the trailhead, return to your vehicle.

As you leave the wildlife area, stop at the planted rows of trees along the entrance road. Each one is identified by name and the year it was planted. You'll see: chokecherry, silver maple, green ash, black walnut, wild plum, and many, many more. You should be impressed by this large display.

Ready for More?
Hike through native prairie at nearby Cayler Prairie State Preserve.

Waterfall Hike
Dunning's Spring Park

Distance: 2.47 miles

Time: 1.75 hours

Path: Rocky dirt path with some steep uphill climbs. The dirt path varies from about six feet wide to one foot wide.

Directions: At the intersection of College Drive and Quarry Street in Decorah, turn northeast onto Quarry (there is a sign). This road takes you to the park entrance; turn left.

Contact: Decorah Parks and Recreation, 400 West Claiborne Drive, Decorah, Iowa 52101; (563) 382-4158. www.decorahparkrec.com

Highlights: A rushing, roaring waterfall, challenging (and fun) hills, and a walk in the wood—a great combo. This is a walk for a day when you have lots of energy and high spirits.

After you've admired the waterfall (walk up the path beside it, in front of it, all around it), it's time to get started on the trails. As you face the waterfall, look to the right. The trailhead sign warns about the high cliffs (stay on the path; don't go beyond the barriers). The rocky trail is four to five feet across and heads uphill immediately. At the first junction, go straight. Ignore the spur trails that visitors have started; it's fairly easy to distinguish them from the official trails.

The path narrows to about two feet as you continue up the steep slope, with a hefty drop-off on the right. Notice the scraggly red cedar along here. Soon you'll come to an overlook with quite a view: Luther College is spread out in front of you. Go straight at the next junction, past a clearing with stately pines. Facing the opposite way is a sign that says Upper Dunning Trail. Just past the sign is another junction; continue to go straight. You'll see some maples, oaks, and hickories.

At about 0.5 mile, turn right at the junction. Wild geranium blooms along the now-wide trail. It's easy to spot deer along here. Notice a steep ravine to the right, along with a boundary fence on the left.

In 0.5 mile, at another junction, go straight (a sign points out that Upper Ice Cave Trail is to the right—don't take it). Now you're immersed in a stand of tall red pine. Just past the boundary fence is a large grassy field.

At the next junction, continue to go straight. Notice the big ravine

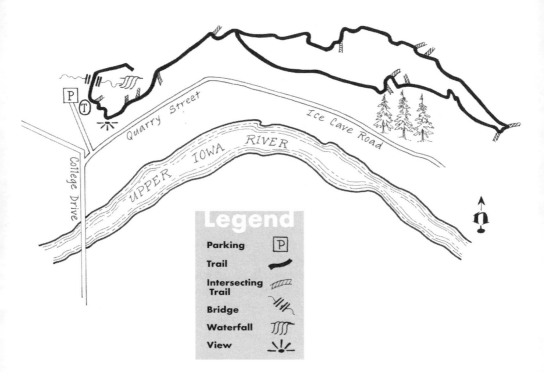

Legend

Parking 🅿

Trail

Intersecting Trail

Bridge

Waterfall

View

on the left now. You'll be winding through trees; a few small branches rain down on a windy day. You won't see many pines at the moment. A barbed-wire fence runs along the ravine on the left. Also notice the large white oak trees (and maple leaves in the litter) on the path. Now there is a ravine to the left and a steep slope on the right—and the fence has disappeared.

At about 1 mile, notice the north-facing slopes with lots of ferns and some wildflowers. And it's downhill as far as you can see on the path, which widens to about six feet. At the next junction, go straight. (A sign to the left says: No Horses, Decorah Parks and Recreation.) Almost immediately, another trail takes off on the left; continue straight. Now you'll start an uphill climb as the trail curves to the right. In summer, notice Virginia waterleaf on the slope to your right. The path narrows to about two feet in width. Moss grows on several large rocks.

When you've gone another 0.25 mile and reached the next junction, bear right. (Straight ahead leads to a road, which you don't want.) After the turn, you'll still be climbing—this is a switchback of sorts. As you walk the switchback, a sign at the next junction tells you this is Backside Trail—which continues straight at this intersection (don't turn left). The path narrows to about a foot wide—and you're still ascending. Watch your footing. One misstep and you'll be rolling down the slope—it's just a footfall away. The path can be wet and muddy, especially after a rain, and slick too. Virginia waterleaf still blooms along the path.

At about 1.5 miles, bear left at a junction. Lots of pine here! Stroll beneath huge pine trees, with a carpet of needles and cones beneath your feet. White pine produces the long, curved cones you see scattered on the ground. Go straight at the next junction. Two hundred yards farther, another trail goes left or right—veer right. The pines are still with you along the trail.

Now, at about 1.75 miles, you'll see a sign that faces the opposite way, which says Upper Ice Cave Trail (you didn't take this trail before; now you've looped back to this spot). From here, retrace your steps to the parking area and the waterfall.

Back at the parking area, head north to the small bridge that crosses the end of the falls—and go up about 119 stairs to the viewing platform near the top of the rushing waterfall. Watch the spring water gush from the cliff and tumble to the ground. Look at red columbine and red cedar growing out of the side of the cliff too.

Not many walks can end with such a flourish. Enjoy the finale.

Wetlands Walk
New Haven Potholes

Distance: 1.71 miles

Time: 52 minutes

Path: Mowed grass and dirt trails.

Directions: Head east on State Highway 9 about 7 miles from Osage and turn left (north) onto Shadow Avenue. The small sign at the intersection, which says New Haven Potholes, is easy to miss. About 1.5 miles down this gravel road, look for the entrance on the right: a driveway leads back about a hundred yards to a signboard and a log building.

Contact: Mitchell County Conservation Board, 18793 State Highway 9, Osage, IA 50461; (641) 732-5204. www.osage.net/~mccb

Highlights: Here, you'll find some interesting wetlands, woods, and even a prairie. This tucked-away "outdoor classroom" offers all three habitats in an easy walk. After a heavy rainfall, some portions of the trail may be flooded.

Begin your walk at the signboard. The board tells you about wetlands in the area: how they were created as the Little Cedar River changed course and isolated old channels, which then filled in with water. (There is a man-made pothole here as well.) The brochures (on the back side of the signboard) contain useful information about the color-coded interpretive trails. This walk doesn't follow any specific trail but wanders the entire area.

The log cabin near the signboard mimics pioneer homes of the past. The cabin isn't open now, nor is the nature center (a new conservation headquarters and nature center was built near Osage). But the trails are fun to walk, as always. And the educational and outdoor classroom programs are still offered here.

The wide, mowed-grass path leads you past the cabin. On your right, notice the barbed-wire fence. Within a few hundred feet you'll see some aspen. At the first junction, continue straight on the path. Soon, the trail loses most of its grass. Along here, you'll see quite a bit of wild geranium. A wet area is off the trail to your left.

At the next junction, continue straight as well; do not cross the small stream on the suspension bridge (if the area has had some flooding, the bridge may not be in good repair). Note the willows on both sides of the bridge. As you continue on, you'll see some natural

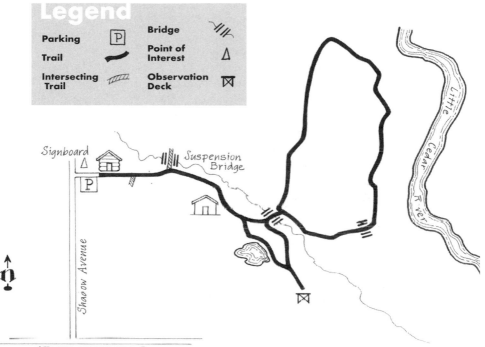

Legend

Parking ⬚P

Trail

Intersecting Trail

Bridge

Point of Interest △

Observation Deck ⊠

Signboard

Suspension Bridge

Shadow Avenue

STATE HIGHWAY 9

rock in the path, which is mostly wet grass and dirt. Shortly, you'll be at the old nature center. This building isn't in use, so just pass by. In summer, pick wild raspberries along here. At a junction just past this building, take the trail to the right. Here, you'll see some box elder trees and lots of leopard frogs on and near the trail in this low area. You'll also see a man-made pond—or pothole—blasted out with dynamite.

Just past this is another junction (do not turn left); continue straight to a large wetland area (the south marsh). The observation deck is a great place to watch waterfowl. (A plaque tells you that it has been dedicated to a local veterinarian who loved the area.) You might see a wood duck, a teal, a mallard, or a Canada goose, and occasionally a sandhill crane.

Notice the silver maple near the observation area. Look for cattails, too, as well as muskrat and beaver. You've walked about 0.5 mile now.

After you've enjoyed the wetlands and observation deck, retrace your steps to the last junction and turn right. Watch for red-tailed hawks as you walk. Huge silver maple trees line the path. At about 0.75 mile, turn right at a junction and cross a wet area on a small wooden plank bridge. Just past the bridge is another intersection; bear left. This area may be under a few inches of water, depending on the season and weather.

Now you'll be walking in a more open, grassy area. Here, even if it's not underwater, each step might be squishy. You'll see lots of frogs on and near the path and some basswood.

As you enter a wooded area with pockets of water, be prepared for mosquitoes. Because it's so wet, you can easily see deer tracks—lots of them. There are quite a few snags in the woods too. Soon you'll walk by a large silver maple—wow. It's surrounded by water, and it's huge. Because this is a wetland, prone to flooding, you'll see piles of washed-up trees and brush. This isn't a postcard-pretty woods, but it's natural and interesting.

At about 1.25 miles, don't get sidetracked by the deer trails that take off in several directions; stay on the same path, which veers to the right. Look for bur oak as you walk. Next is a small plank bridge, which takes you past a water-control structure. You've walked about 1.35 miles to this point. Soon after this, you've completed a loop and are back at a familiar intersection. From here, head west, then north-west, and retrace your steps back to the signboard and the beginning of your walk.

Ready for More?
Grab the prairie brochure and walk a prairie loop.

Urban Strolls

Dubuque's Riverwalk

River City Sights
Mason City

Distance: 3.17 miles

Time: 2 hours

Path: City sidewalk, asphalt path, and grass. An easy urban stroll.

Directions: From State Highway 122 in Mason City, turn north onto Pennsylvania Avenue in the downtown area. After you cross the bridge on Pennsylvania, note that the boyhood home of Meredith Willson (composer of *The Music Man*), and Music Man Square will be on the west side of the street. Turn into the parking lot in front of the Mason City Public Library to the east.

Contact: None. For more info about city attractions contact the Mason City Convention and Visitor's Bureau, 25 West State Street, Mason City, IA 50401-1128; (800) 423-5724. www.masoncitytourism.com

Highlights: Stroll through "River City," with a stop at the library, a museum, across Meredith Willson/Music Man Footbridge, and through a city park. Admire the Frank Lloyd Wright Stockman House, then head for Music Man Square and Willson's boyhood home. When you're done with your walk, stop at Marjorie's Tea House for lunch.

Begin your walk from the parking lot in front of the Mason City Public Library. Step inside the library and head for the reading room; the whole back wall is a bank of windows that overlooks the library's woodland path, a wonderful spot behind the library that you can walk, which is where you're headed next. First, take a peek at the cheery, unique room in the children's section. Padded benches form a semicircle along an outside wall, and windows above the seating let in tons of light. The room is big enough to let a child's imagination soar, and cozy enough to settle in with a good book. Here, you can see the wooded path behind the library too.

After you've wandered the library, walk outside to the northeast edge of the building and look for the asphalt path behind the library. (Ask inside the library if you don't see it.) Walk down about five stone steps to a bench—the perfect vantage point to sit and gaze at the greenery below—or immerse yourself in a good book from the library. Although the space behind the library is sometimes referred to as the "library gardens," you won't find a manicured garden, but a lovely little green space with wildflowers and a shaded woodland path that winds along a creek. Continue down about 26 railroad-tie steps

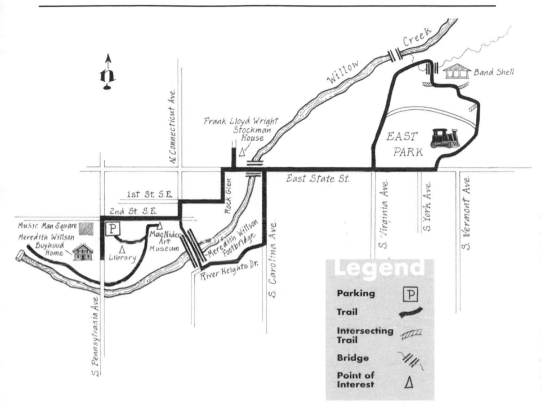

to reach the asphalt path again. Now you are below the library building. Notice some rock outcroppings to the right, along with box elder and maple trees.

At the T-intersection bear right (straight ahead would take you into Willow Creek) and follow the path along the creek. This path changes to grass through a small clearing; then you'll pick up an asphalt trail again. Cottonwoods and silver maples decorate Willow Creek's banks. Follow the creek to the dam (about 0.25 mile), your turnaround point. Retrace your steps to the library and continue your walk.

Now walk (east) toward the Charles H. MacNider Art Museum next door. Take the shortcut on a walkway between the two buildings. Inside the museum, a painting of General Hanford MacNider greets you on the first floor. (The museum was a gift to the city from the MacNider family.) Admire Grant Wood's art. Then wander upstairs to a cozy reading room and the Bil Baird World of Puppets. Check out the modern art display before you descend a winding staircase. If you're passionate about architecture, the Mason City Walking Tour Guide is available here (for a fee). The booklet guides you around nearby neighborhoods and discusses architectural style, including a home designed by Frank Lloyd Wright and more.

When you've finished perusing art at the museum, continue on the

Take a stroll across the Meredith Willson/Music Man
Footbridge in Mason City.

city sidewalk in an easterly direction toward the Meredith Willson/
Music Man Footbridge. Willson's boyhood home is just a few blocks
away. Mason City is known as the inspiration behind the fictitious
"River City" in Willson's well-known musical, *The Music Man*. During Mason City's annual North Iowa Band Festival in the spring,
you'll even see banners around town that say "Welcome to River City."

As you cross the bridge, look at the sheer rock wall below, to your
right, jutting up from Willow Creek. Here, the bridge skims along
some treetops: silver maple and red oak. Look down; you'll also see
some cottonwood below the bridge.

Turn left onto River Heights Drive. Pay attention to some of the
architectural styles of the homes along here. (The Mason City Walking Tour Guide can provide lots of details.) At the intersection with
South Carolina Avenue, cross the street and walk on the right side of
South Carolina Avenue, also known as Carolina Hill. At the bottom

of the hill, turn right (east) onto East State Street. If you visit Mason City during the weekend of the North Iowa Band Festival, this is a great spot to watch the parade unfold in front of you. You've walked slightly more than 1 mile to this point.

Enjoy the architectural style of the homes along East State Street as well (also mentioned in the Mason City Walking Tour Guide). Notice the plaques in the sidewalk in front of several homes that will help you identify the unique structures.

Continue on East State Street for another 0.5 mile. Just past South York Avenue, cross East State Street to the East Park entrance. Follow the entrance road past a huge play area for kids and an old steam locomotive. The road veers to the left and winds through the park. Cross the park road and take the asphalt path that leads you past an old-fashioned band shell with rows of wooden benches in front of it. It's still the site of many musical events today. Then return to the wide asphalt path and turn right to go across a stone footbridge.

After the bridge, head toward the park road to the left. Cross the street and walk along the side of Willow Creek. As you walk along the retaining wall near the creek, you'll see another footbridge to the right called East Park Footbridge/The Music Man/ Laminated Wood Arch. (There is a marker set in the ground at this spot.) Walk partway across the bridge; admire the view and return to the same path. It's a lovely spot; many wedding and graduation pictures have been taken on or near this bridge.

Now cross the street and walk near the tennis courts. At the corner of East State Street and South Virginia Avenue, turn right (west) and continue on. You're walking on the other side of East State Street now. Enjoy the architectural styles of the stately homes on this shaded, tree-lined street. If you're visiting during the weekend of the North Iowa Band Festival, traffic along East State can be heavy; other times of the year it's a quiet, relaxing stroll.

In about 0.5 mile, you'll cross Willow Creek again on a cement bridge. To the right is the Frank Lloyd Wright Stockman House (at the intersection of 1st Street NE and East State Street). After you've admired the Prairie School design, turn left (south) onto Rock Glen. Follow the next curve up a slight hill (now 1st Street SE) to South Connecticut Avenue. Go south here, passing the footbridge, the museum, and the library on your way to Music Man Square.

A statue of Meredith Willson tipping his hat is the first thing you'll notice. At Music Man Square, step inside and walk along the 1912 River City Streetscape (which is just like River City in *The Music Man*). Visit the museum and tour Willson's boyhood home too. By the time you leave, you'll be humming "76 Trombones."

Stop at Marjorie's Tea House next door, also part of the Music Man Square complex.

Riverwalk and Port of Dubuque
Dubuque

Distance: 4.79 miles (plus a downtown stroll)

Time: 2 hours or more

Path: Decorative paved path, asphalt, city street. The multihued Riverwalk path is a pleasure to walk, leading you to scenic spots and stops along America's River. Walk beneath the Julien Dubuque Bridge and up on the levee too.

Directions: From U.S. Highway 20 in Dubuque, turn north on Locust Street toward the downtown area. Turn right (east) onto West 3rd Street. You'll pass by the Iowa Welcome Center to your left. Continue past Main Street and over a bridge. Now you're on East 3rd Street. (You'll see the National Mississippi River Museum and Aquarium on the right.) Turn left onto Bell Street, past the Grand Harbor Resort and Waterpark and then the Grand River Center (on your right). At the T-intersection (it's a dead-end straight ahead), turn left into a parking lot. The Grand River Center parking is to the right.

Contact: None. For area information, contact the Iowa Welcome Center/ Visitor Information, 300 Main Street, Suite 100, Dubuque, IA 52001; (563) 556-4372 or (800) 798-8444. www.traveldubuque.com

Highlights: Enjoy the sights and sounds of the Port of Dubuque as you stroll the unique Riverwalk and beyond. Gaze at the Shot Tower, meander through the amphitheater, go up on the levee, and down by the docks. Dip your toes into the Mississippi. Walk beneath the Julien Dubuque Bridge. When you're done rambling along the river, take a trolley or carriage ride through the historic downtown district. Stop at Fenelon Place Elevator Company and ride a cable car up a short, steep hill—with gorgeous views at the top.

Begin your walk at the Alliant Energy Amphitheater, northeast of the parking lot and just below the Riverwalk. The outdoor amphitheater's unique half-circle seating, adjacent to the flood wall, faces the old Dubuque Star Brewery. The brewery remains closed today, but the massive brick building is still a great backdrop for concerts and other outdoor events.

As you walk across the decorative, concrete arena, notice the large star that radiates from the center of its design. Just past the brewery is the Shot Tower, a well-known Dubuque landmark. Built in 1856, the tower was able to produce literally tons of lead shot. Imagine lead, heated and then poured from the top of the tower, making its way

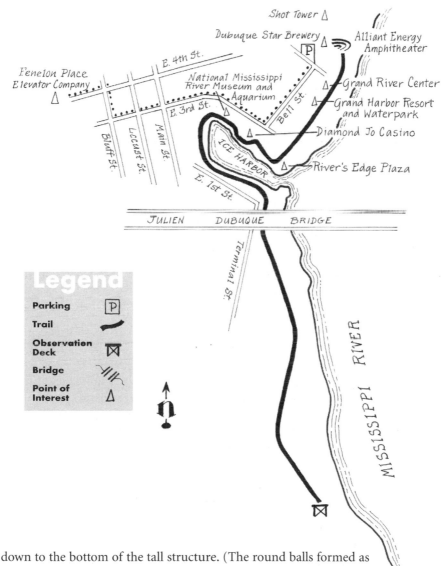

Legend

Parking [P]

Trail

Observation Deck

Bridge

Point of Interest △

down to the bottom of the tall structure. (The round balls formed as lead passed through screens along the way.)

Near the end of the amphitheater, turn right and go up a series of steps to reach the Riverwalk. At the top, look out across the vast Mississippi and at the swing bridge. (A swing bridge opens to let river traffic pass through.) This also is a good vantage point to view the Dubuque Star Brewery and Shot Tower (which is on the right now).

As you stroll the Riverwalk, enjoy the breeze on top of the flood-wall and watch for a great blue heron rising from the water. Along the path you can browse the signboards, which offer bits and pieces of Dubuque's history. Take advantage of the well-placed benches for a few minutes of contemplation or just to people-watch. Families, locals, visitors, and couples of all ages are out and about. The Grand River Center's glass-paneled room juts out over the Riverwalk toward the river, mirroring the sky and the clouds. You'll also walk by the Grand Harbor Resort and Waterpark, another component of the America's River project that has reenergized the port.

Gawk at the Julien Dubuque Bridge, stretching across the Mississippi. Julien Dubuque, the city's namesake, is thought to have been the first European to settle in Iowa. A monument marking his grave, which lies high above the Mississippi, can be seen at the Mines of Spain State Recreation Area.

When you reach the open pavilion of River's Edge Plaza, take the steps that lead to the water's edge and dip your toes or fingers in the mighty Mississippi. Boaters can dock near here, an easy way for them to join in the activity at the Port of Dubuque.

After you pass through the floodgate, look for the *Spirit of Dubuque*, an authentic, festive paddle wheeler that can take you for a spin on the river. River cruises on other vessels are also available at Ice Harbor. Continue on the path as it passes in front of the *Diamond Jo Casino*. Stop for the slots, too, if you wish.

Soon you'll be at the National Mississippi River Museum and Aquarium. It's a gem! A large paddle wheel spins near the museum's entrance. Spend an hour or a half-day here: gaze at gators, walk a wetland trail, and get to know the Mississippi intimately through hands-on displays, aquariums, and more. Through the museum, you can tour the *William M. Black*, a dredge boat listed on the National Register of Historic Places. It's even possible to stay overnight on the boat on certain days (it's called the "Boat and Breakfast" option). Stop by the Depot Café (an actual refurbished depot) while visiting the museum, too.

After you've scoured the museum and aquarium, follow the distinctive path around the corner, heading east now. Here, you'll get a good side view of the *William M. Black*.

Although the decorative pathway ends at the next corner, your walk does not. (You've walked about 1 mile to this point.) Follow the city street as it wraps around the other side of Ice Harbor. When the street dead-ends, turn right in a southerly direction. There isn't much to look at along this stretch once you're past the harbor. But soon you're walking beneath the Julien Dubuque Bridge—and it's impressive from any angle.

Continue on for about 0.25 mile until you reach the levee. Next to a small parking area, an asphalt path leads up to the top of the floodwall. Dozens of turkey vultures camp out near the water, along with some herons. The river widens here, and you get a sense of the enormous power of this waterway.

Take a break from your walk and ride the Fenelon Place cable car for a grand view of Dubuque and the Mississippi River.

This levee walk is popular: you'll see cyclists, couples out for a leisurely stroll, dogs and their owners, and some joggers. A viewing platform at your turnaround point is another scenic spot—take advantage of the views. You've walked almost 2.5 miles to this point. Fill your eyes with the Mississippi, then retrace your steps along the levee, back to the Riverwalk, past the amphitheater, and to your car. Look for mud turtles on the way back.

When you're through exploring the paths near the river, head to the historic downtown district, just minutes away. Walk, drive, take the trolley or even a carriage (pickup locations are nearby; the Iowa Welcome Center has information and brochures). Stop at the Fenelon Place Elevator Company (on the National Register of Historic Places) and ride a cable car up the short, steep incline. At the top, you'll have a sweeping view of three states (Iowa, Illinois, and Wisconsin). Pick

179

up the brochure, which tells the story of a man who wanted a quicker way to get to his home on top of the bluffs so he would have enough time for lunch and a nap.

Peruse the Victorian architecture as you wander the area. Stop by Café Manna Java on Main Street. The signature sandwiches and artisan breads are wonderful. Try the "Sofia," cranberry walnut bread with apple butter, cheeses, and chicken.

Ready for More?

Hop on one of many hiking trails at the Mines of Spain State Recreation Area—and visit the Julien Dubuque Monument.

MORE GREAT TITLES
FROM TRAILS BOOKS
& PRAIRIE OAK PRESS

ACTIVITY GUIDES

Biking Wisconsin: 50 Great Road and Trail Rides, *Steve Johnson*

Great Cross-Country Ski Trails: Wisconsin, Minnesota, Michigan & Ontario, *Wm. Chad McGrath*

Great Iowa Walks: 50 Strolls, Rambles, Hikes, and Treks, *Lynn L. Walters*

Great Minnesota Walks: 49 Strolls, Rambles, Hikes, and Treks, *Wm. Chad McGrath*

Great Wisconsin Walks: 45 Strolls, Rambles, Hikes, and Treks, *Wm. Chad McGrath*

Horsing Around in Wisconsin, *Anne M. Connor*

Iowa Underground, *Greg A. Brick*

Minnesota Underground & the Best of the Black Hills, *Doris Green*

Paddling Illinois: 64 Great Trips by Canoe and Kayak, *Mike Svob*

Paddling Iowa: 96 Great Trips by Canoe and Kayak, *Nate Hoogeveen*

Paddling Northern Minnesota: 86 Great Trips by Canoe and Kayak, *Lynne Smith Diebel*

Paddling Northern Wisconsin: 82 Great Trips by Canoe and Kayak, *Mike Svob*

Paddling Southern Wisconsin: 82 Great Trips by Canoe and Kayak, *Mike Svob*

Walking Tours of Wisconsin's Historic Towns, *Lucy Rhodes, Elizabeth McBride, Anita Matcha*

Wisconsin's Outdoor Treasures: A Guide to 150 Natural Destinations, *Tim Bewer*

Wisconsin Underground, *Doris Green*

TRAVEL GUIDES

Classic Wisconsin Weekends, *Michael Bie*

Great Little Museums of the Midwest, *Christine des Garennes*

Great Midwest Country Escapes, *Nina Gadomski*

Great Minnesota Taverns, *David K. Wright & Monica G. Wright*

Great Minnesota Weekend Adventures, *Beth Gauper*

Great Weekend Adventures, *the Editors of Wisconsin Trails*

Great Wisconsin Romantic Weekends, *Christine des Garennes*

Great Wisconsin Taverns: 101 Distinctive Badger Bars, *Dennis Boyer*

Iowa's Hometown Flavors, *Donna Tabbert Long*

Sacred Sites of Minnesota, *John-Brian Paprock & Teresa Peneguy Paprock*

Sacred Sites of Wisconsin, *John-Brian Paprock & Teresa Peneguy Paprock*

Tastes of Minnesota: A Food Lover's Tour, *Donna Tabbert Long*

The Great Iowa Touring Book: 27 Spectacular Auto Trips, *Mike Whye*

The Great Minnesota Touring Book: 30 Spectacular Auto Trips, *Thomas Huhti*

The Great Wisconsin Touring Book: 30 Spectacular Auto Tours, *Gary Knowles*

Wisconsin Family Weekends: 20 Fun Trips for You and the Kids, *Susan Lampert Smith*

Wisconsin Golf Getaways, *Jeff Mayers and Jerry Poling*

Wisconsin Lighthouses: A Photographic and Historical Guide,
Ken and Barb Wardius
Wisconsin's Hometown Flavors, *Terese Allen*
Wisconsin Waterfalls, *Patrick Lisi*
Up North Wisconsin: A Region for All Seasons, *Sharyn Alden*

HOME & GARDEN
Bountiful Wisconsin: 110 Favorite Recipes, *Terese Allen*
Codfather 2, *Jeff Hagen*
Creating a Perennial Garden in the Midwest, *Joan Severa*
Eating Well in Wisconsin, *Jerry Minnich*
Foods That Made Wisconsin Famous: 150 Great Recipes, *Richard J. Baumann*
Midwest Cottage Gardening, *Frances Manos*
North Woods Cottage Cookbook, *Jerry Minnich*
Wisconsin Country Gourmet, *Marge Snyder & Suzanne Breckenridge*
Wisconsin Garden Guide, *Jerry Minnich*

HISTORICAL BOOKS
Barns of Wisconsin, *Jerry Apps*
Duck Hunting on the Fox: Hunting and Decoy-Carving Traditions,
Stephen M. Miller
Grand Army of the Republic: Department of Wisconsin, *Thomas J. McCrory*
Portrait of the Past: A Photographic Journey Through Wisconsin 1865-1920,
Howard Mead, Jill Dean, and Susan Smith
Prairie Whistles: Tales of Midwest Railroading, *Dennis Boyer*
Shipwrecks of Lake Michigan, *Benjamin J. Shelak*
Wisconsin At War: 20th Century Conflicts Through the Eyes of Veterans, *Dr. James
F. McIntosh, M.D.*
Wisconsin's Historic Houses & Living History Museums, *Krista Finstad Hanson*
Wisconsin: The Story of the Badger State, *Norman K. Risjord*

GIFT BOOKS
Celebrating Door County's Wild Places, *The Ridges Sanctuary*
Fairlawn: Restoring the Splendor, *Tom Davis*
Madison, *Photography by Brent Nicastro*
Milwaukee, *Photography by Todd Dacquisto*
Milwaukee Architecture: A Guide to Notable Buildings, *Joseph Korom*
Spirit of the North: A Photographic Journey Through Northern Wisconsin, *Richard
Hamilton Smith*
The Spirit of Door County: A Photographic Essay, *Darryl R. Beers*
Uncommon Sense: The Life Of Marshall Erdman, *Doug Moe & Alice D'Alessio*

LEGENDS & LORE
Driftless Spirits: Ghosts of Southwest Wisconsin, *Dennis Boyer*
Haunted Wisconsin, *Michael Norman and Beth Scott*

The Beast of Bray Road: Tailing Wisconsin's Werewolf, *Linda S. Godfrey*
The Eagle's Voice: Tales Told by Indian Effigy Mounds, *Gary J. Maier, M.D.*
The Poison Widow: A True Story of Sin, Strychnine, & Murder, *Linda S. Godfrey*
The W-Files: True Reports of Wisconsin's Unexplained Phenomena, *Jay Rath*

YOUNG READERS

ABCs Naturally, *Lynne Smith Diebel & Jann Faust Kalscheur*
ABCs of Wisconsin, *Dori Hillestad Butler, Illustrated by Alison Relyea*
H is for Hawkeye, *Jay Wagner, Illustrated by Eileen Potts Dawson*
H is for Hoosier, *Dori Hillestad Butler, Illustrated by Eileen Potts Dawson*
Wisconsin Portraits, *Martin Hintz*
Wisconsin Sports Heroes, *Martin Hintz*
W is for Wisconsin, *Dori Hillestad Butler, Illustrated by Eileen Potts Dawson*

SPORTS

Baseball in Beertown: America's Pastime in Milwaukee, *Todd Mishler*
Before They Were the Packers: Green Bay's Town Team Days,
Denis J. Gullickson & Carl Hanson
Cold Wars: 40+ Years of Packer-Viking Rivalry, *Todd Mishler*
Downfield: Untold Stories of the Green Bay Packers, *Jerry Poling*
Great Moments in Wisconsin Sports, *Todd Mishler*
Green Bay Packers Titletown Trivia Teasers, *Don Davenport*
Mean on Sunday: The Autobiography of Ray Nitschke, *Robert W. Wells*
Mudbaths and Bloodbaths: The Inside Story of the Bears-Packers Rivalry,
Gary D'Amato & Cliff Christl
Packers By the Numbers: Jersey Numbers and the Players Who Wore Them,
John Maxymuk

OTHER

Driftless Stories, *John Motoviloff*
River Stories: Growing Up on the Wisconsin, *Delores Chamberlain*
The Wisconsin Father's Guide to Divorce, *James Novak*
Travels With Sophie: The Journal of Louise E. Wegner,
Edited by Gene L. LaBerge & Michelle L. Maurer
Trout Friends, *Bill Stokes*
Wild Wisconsin Notebook, *James Buchholz*

For a free catalog, phone, write, or e-mail us.

Trails Books

P.O. Box 317, Black Earth, WI 53515
(800) 236-8088 • e-mail: books@wistrails.com